I0555434

What Readers Are Saying about *A Mother Like Me*

"Angie's book is a very personal, intimate look at the death of her precious son, Kevin. Obviously, her journey has been undergirded by her faith. Other faith-based, bereaved parents can find hope for healing in her willingness to open her heart and express her grief into authentic mourning. I admire her willingness to put her pen to paper. Keep the faith, Angie!"

—Dr. Alan Wolfelt, PhD, CT, Author,
Director of the Center for Loss and Life Transition

"There are no words to describe the beauty of Angie's writing of such a difficult subject. She brings tears, joy, love, sadness, faith, and pain together. She is giving a beautiful gift to others who have lost a child, and for those grieving with friends and family members who have lost a loved one. Once I started reading, I couldn't stop. I cannot wait to read more of her writing. She has a gift, and I hope this will not be her last book."

—Judy Cunningham, Author, Artist,
Master in Educational Leadership

"Angie's book is an amazing resource for those who have suffered the loss of a child or are supporting someone in this tragic situation. It can feel impossible to describe the type of pain and anguish which comes with any tragedy, let alone the loss of a child. Angie has braved her own journey and in choosing to share it she provides the language needed to survive and heal from the unimaginable."

—Monica Nevarez, MSW, ACSW

"*A Mother Like Me* is a moving narrative of one woman's journey through grief. I read it in a single sitting. I have not experienced that most grave and terrible wound of losing a child, so I can't know what Angie knows. I can only imagine. Reading this story of pain, courage, grace, and hope was a blessing to me, and I think any mother would relate to it, and learn from it. Angie's writing style is genuine and lovely."

—Anne Lukens Underwood, Author

"This is a powerful, incredible, and insightful work! Angie's writing is like personally being there with her and feeling the raw emotions as she reveals all that's happened."   —Joni Wilson, Editor

A MOTHER LIKE ME

A Story of Faith,
Hope, and Love
in Loss

ANGIE FORD-GREEN

© 2023 by Angie Ford-Green. All rights reserved.

All rights reserved. Except in the case of brief quotations embodied in critical articles and reviews, no portion of this book may be reproduced, stored in a retrieval system, or transmitted in any form or by any means—electronic, mechanical, photocopy, recording, scanning, or other—without the prior written permission from the author. None of the material in this book may be reproduced for any commercial promotion, advertising, or sale of a product or service.

While the author has made every effort to provide accurate internet addresses at the time of publication, neither the publisher nor the author assumes any responsibility for errors or for changes that occur after publication. Further, the publisher does not have any control over and does not assume any responsibility for author or third-party websites or their content.

ISBN: 979-8-2182911-9-8 (Paperback)

Published by

 Sunflower Books and Art
sunflowerbooksandart@gmail.com

Editing by Adam Colwell's WriteWorks, LLC, Adam Colwell and Ginger Colwell
Copyediting by Joni Wilson
Cover and interior design by Deborah Perdue, Illumination Graphics
Printed in the United States of America

Bible Versions Used in This Book
AMP, American Standard Version. Copyright © 2015 by The Lockman Foundation, La Habra, CA 90631. All rights reserved.

BSB, Berean Study Bible. Public Domain.

ESV, English Standard Version. The Holy Bible, English Standard Version. ESV® Text Edition: 2016. Copyright © 2001 by Crossway Bibles, a publishing ministry of Good News Publishers.

KJV, King James Version. Public Domain.

NASB, New American Standard Bible. New American Standard Bible®, Copyright © 1960, 1971, 1977, 1995, 2020 by The Lockman Foundation. All rights reserved.

NIV, New International Version. Holy Bible, New International Version®, NIV® Copyright ©1973, 1978, 1984, 2011 by Biblica, Inc.® Used by permission. All rights reserved worldwide.

NKJV, New King James Version. Scripture taken from the New King James Version®. Copyright © 1982 by Thomas Nelson. Used by permission. All rights reserved.

NLT, New Living Translation. Holy Bible, New Living Translation, copyright © 1996, 2004, 2015 by Tyndale House Foundation. Used by permission of Tyndale House Publishers, Inc., Carol Stream, Illinois 60188. All rights reserved.

Contents

Symbolism of the Sand Dollar

Sand dollars represent rebirth, renewal, and transformation due to their unique life cycle. In many cultures, they depict the birth, death, and resurrection of Jesus Christ. The small holes symbolize Jesus' wounds from being nailed to the Cross.

In Loving Memory of Our Son

Kevin Russell Green

December 8, 1973—January 10, 2002

A Beautiful Soul
Handsome, Gentle, Kind, Loving, Fun, Funny, Full of Life

Thank you, God, for this light. This warming fire that leaned against us and touched our very souls. You will be in our hearts always, Luvvy. We will miss you every day until the day we meet again in Heaven, where we will stand together in Christ forever and ever and ever . . .

"When someone you love becomes a memory, that memory becomes a treasure."
—Unknown

Dedication

For My Sons, Eric, David, and Kevin.

Foreword

"God, enlarge me through my loss and use it to bring hope to others . . . that multiplies!"

THIS WAS MY HEART'S CRY YEARS AGO IN THE MIDST of gut-wrenching grief, after suffering through infertility; miscarriages; carrying my son, John Samuel, with a fatal birth defect; and losing him shortly after birth. Little did I know then that God would use my journey of suffering and loss to open doors for me to write, speak, and to start a Hopelifters ministry to touch multitudes of hurting people around the world.

Amazingly, in 2019, God connected me to Angie, a mom like me, and seasoned sufferer in the journey. Our online friendship ignited, and we discovered we share a passion to use our pain for God's purpose, spread hope from our hurt and help others to do the same. We also share an "iron spirit" and "marathon mentality" to persevere in God's power and finish well.

When Angie shared her dream for this book, *A Mother Like Me*, I was thrilled to cheer her on to see her dream become a reality. Angie's book is an authentic, heartfelt, personal journey of grief, and how the ripple effects of loss touches an entire family. Sharing deeply from her heart, Angie gives you permission to plummet to the depths of unthinkable pain and experience God's compassion and hope through your own personal journey. Angie's words are a companion of hope—you are not alone in your grief, and you will make it through your loss.

A Mother Like Me can also be given as a gift or encouraging tool to spread hope to others on a similar journey of grieving a loss or for those who want to help others. Think of this book as a trusted companion to encourage you or others to suffer deeply and well like Angie and me.

You are not alone in your grief. My prayer is in God's strength and timing, you will also share your story to someone who might feel alone and needs hope.

Turn the page and be encouraged . . . Cheering you on,
—Kathe Wunnenberg, Author, Speaker, Founder of
Hopelifters Unlimited
Grieving the Child I Never Knew
Grieving the Loss of a Loved One
Hopelifter: Creative Ways to Spread Hope
When Life Hurts

Preface

"Write in a book all the words I have spoken to you."
(Jeremiah 30:2, NIV)

SINCE THE 1960S USHERED IN A SOCIAL AND SEXUAL revolution, there has been a lot of speculation and talk about spirituality and the spiritual realm. Unfortunately, there has also been an increasing number of people who consider themselves spiritual, while denying the existence of a Divine and Sovereign Creator God.

I write this book as a testament of praise that God indeed exists. I have experienced His presence and loving movements and actions throughout my life, most profoundly during the times I have spent in the shadows of death and the fires of unexpected sorrow.

My heartfelt and fervent prayer is that *A Mother Like Me* will encourage you to consider, seek, and discover the reality of a Divine, Holy, and Loving God. It is also my hope that you will draw close to Him to experience His unfailing, never-ending compassion, comfort, mercy, and grace in your brokenness, despair, and seasons of grief.

As a precious friend and author, Jodi Rosser, writes in her book, *Depth: Growing through Heartbreak to Strength*, "Heartbreak comes when life does not end up the way you planned or expected. These disappointments are very real and can leave you feeling like there is a deep hole in your soul. Grief is the hardest emotion to navigate. God redeems the pain. The depth in your life is one of the greatest gifts in the middle of the heartbreak." Jodi encourages and inspires others to "grow deeper in their faith, and to find hope and purpose through their unexpected storms."

During my journey of grief after the sudden cardiac death of our youngest son, Kevin, I learned an important truth: God does not hide from us or intentionally keep His love, comfort, and healing power from us. He is not stingy with His love and mercy, and His promise to never forsake or leave us is true for anyone who believes and calls upon His Name.

I wish I could sit and visit with you, hearing about your loss and how you are doing. I'm glad you have picked up my book. May a glimpse of my heartache, grief, and intimate relationship with God speak into the deepest part of your heart and soul. Healing from heartbreak is yours. It's up to you to discover it.

"After you have suffered a little while, the God of all grace, who has called you to his eternal glory in Christ, will himself restore, confirm, strengthen, and establish you."

(1 Peter 5:10, ESV)

Holy Grief

The tunnel of grief is a holy place,
A cavern of wisdom and care.
A setting to meet God face to face,
And share every shred of despair.

Priorities change from the burden of grief,
We shed our familiar façade.
Our souls in search of pain's relief
Discover a hunger for God.

With eyes dimmed by tears we catch a view
Of life as it's meant to be.
A sorrowing soul can be renewed,
And sadness can set it free.

So look for revival that only flows
From rivers of sorrow and pain.
And reach for the Lord as one who knows
The holiness that grief can attain.

—Kenneth M. Hekman, *Treasures of Darkness*

"He has sent me to bind up the brokenhearted . . . to comfort all who mourn . . . to bestow on them a crown of beauty instead of ashes, the oil of joy instead of mourning, and a garment of praise instead of a spirit of despair. beauty for ashes, the oil of joy for mourning, praise for the spirit of heaviness that they might be called trees of righteousness, the planting of the LORD that He might be glorified."

(Isaiah 61:3, ESV)

Introduction

"The depths within one word can contain many levels of meaning. The LORD says, choose only the word stones I tell you, and when to hurl them onto the page. Then the words He gives me can have the power of boulders or the tenderness of feathers, I may even hurl them at a giant of unbelief."

—Jan Voth Dubbs, *The Silver Pen*

WORDS—MORE SPECIFICALLY, THE MEANINGS OF words and names—matter very much to me. It is important for me to know the root meaning of words and to choose the right word to express my thoughts and feelings to articulate precisely what I want to communicate.

My parents named me Angela, which means "messenger." When my husband, Bob, and I chose names for our three sons, we chose their names with the hope they would represent the meaning of their name as adults. Our oldest son's name is Eric, and it means "kingly power." David means "beloved." Kevin means "handsome, gentle and kind." Each of them grew into the meaning of their names perfectly.

There's something very special about how words can draw pictures in our minds. As someone who admires people who have "a way with words," I can't imagine what the world would be like without the written word, stories, and books. Spending time in a library or a bookstore is time well spent. As I thumb through the pages of a book, I like to feel the texture of the paper and imagine how the typed word might have once been written by someone using a feather quill pen dipped in an inkwell with pigment residue on their fingers. Those writers are my literary heroes. Books transport me to another place and another time in a way nothing else can. Reading something written by a creative, talented, and skilled storyteller entertains, inspires, and nourishes me. As I apply a well-crafted story, it usually becomes part of my story, adding a new dimension to my life from the writer's vantage point and experiences.

For me, the most creative, inspiring, and nourishing book ever written is the Bible—the God-breathed, inerrant, alive, and active Word. Every moment spent reading, studying, and meditating on God's Word provides fresh, new insight, knowledge, and understanding of God and His love, goodness, and redemptive plan for mankind. The Bible is truly the "lamp unto my feet, and a light unto my path" (Psalm 119:105, KJV).

When considering the possibility of writing a book in

my golden years, I thought of the biblical account of Sarah, Abraham's wife. Genesis 18:15 tells us the LORD (I capitalize the word here to retain its meaning as indicating the Father, Son, and Holy Spirit) had been speaking to Abraham, fully aware that Sarah, nearby inside their tent, was hearing every word. In this conversation, He told Abraham for the second time, and Sarah for the first time, she would have a son by the following year.

When Sarah laughed out loud, the LORD knew why she laughed. In response to her laughter, He told her nothing was too hard or impossible for Him as LORD. Recalling this passage, and how Sarah did indeed conceive and give birth to a son, Isaac, at 90 years of age, I laughed at the idea of writing and publishing a book in my seventies. Feel free to call me "Sarah!"

Having written and blogged for business, education, and ministry for decades, there were many times I thought about a writing career, beginning as far back as the 1960s. The published authors I've met have told me things like, "Writing is tedious," or "It's the most challenging thing I have ever done!" There is truth in what they say—but the most challenging thing I have ever faced had nothing to do with writing, but surviving the fires of unexpected sorrow and making my way through *"the valley of the shadow of death"* (Psalm 23:4, KJV) after my son, Kevin, died in January 2002.

It was after Kevin's death that writing and my grief began to merge, culminating in *A Mother Like Me*. This was not a natural progression, and I often struggled with the process of writing, editing, and publishing. A cursory Google search in 2019 revealed the number of books published each year to be anywhere from 500,000 to one million. Including self-published books, that number rose to four million new book titles annually. *Who am I to think I might have something original to share that could be helpful to someone grieving?*

Then I remembered books most helpful to me in my season of grief were not written by best-selling authors or authorities on grief but by ordinary people sharing real, extraordinary stories of their loss. Yet as I considered writing about my journey through grief, it was a challenge to decide how "real" I wanted to be and what to keep private.

After looking through my bookshelves at home for *The Velveteen Rabbit* by Margery Williams, I searched through the book for a descriptive paragraph about being real.

"Real isn't how you are made," said the Skin Horse. 'It's a thing that happens to you. When a child loves you for a long, long time, not just to play with, but REALLY loves you, then you become Real."

That was it. My sons have loved me "for a long,

long time," and their love for me has made me real. To suffer the loss of my son, Kevin, cast me into the fires of unexpected sorrow, burning away anything pretentious, shallow, superficial, or fake.

A *Mother Like Me* is written for all who grieve the loss of someone they love, but especially for mothers who have suffered and live with the loss of a child every day of their lives.

May my carefully chosen words be of comfort and help to you, and may they be acceptable and pleasing to the LORD (Psalm 19:14).

CHAPTER ONE

A Fairy Tale

"You can make many plans, but the LORD's purpose will prevail."   (Proverbs 19:21, NLT)

MY LIFE BEGAN LIKE A FAIRY TALE. A post-World War II baby, I was born in October 1947 at a time when my grandmother said, "There was a light in every window, a chicken in every pot, and hope in every heart." I was blissfully innocent. There was love and affection between my parents; my brother, Rusty; and me. It was a happy, beautiful childhood. There was no trauma in my young years. So far as I knew, there was no evil, no wickedness, no fear, no distress in my world.

Much of the reason for that, I'd later learn, was because my parents were determined our family would have Jesus Christ as the center point of our family life. Their love and commitment to each other and their faith and trust in a loving, faithful God were the foundations of our family.

I love the story of how my parents met. My mom, Evelyn, was a pretty, naïve, and romantic 18-year-old enamored with Hollywood and the idea of finding her one true love and living happily ever after. My dad, Paul, was a handsome 20-year-old United States Navy war veteran who fought on a battleship somewhere in the Pacific or Atlantic (he never talked about the war). Coming home the summer of 1946, he went to visit his sister and her husband in Fort Smith, Arkansas.

During one of their visits, Aunt Nell told him, "You have to meet Evelyn. She would be perfect for you."

His response was, "I'm looking for a career not a wife," but he agreed to meet her, and when he did, she certainly got his attention. He told his brother-in-law, Joe, "She is jailbait. There is a lot of woman in that young girl's body."

Three months later, they were married, and anyone who knew my parents thought they were perfect for each other. My dad was the youngest of nine children growing up very poor in southeastern Mississippi in a town that was once no more than a lumber camp. With a childhood home built at the edge of Tallahala Creek, he described his upbringing as being like Mark Twain's story about Huckleberry Finn—he and his eight brothers and sisters were wild and free to roam. My mom once told me he didn't have a decent pair of shoes until he got a job in his early teens. His older brother, Homer, influenced him to get educated, make something of himself, and get out of Mississippi as soon as he could.

My mom was the youngest of three girls, and her sisters insisted she was spoiled. Sheltered and overly protected by her parents, she knew nothing about the real world outside of her home, family, and friends, most of whom were part of their close-knit church family.

Both of my parents were Christians, believing Jesus was the Son of God, Emmanuel—God in the flesh, who came to earth and sacrificed His life so all who believe and follow Him will be forgiven of their sins, redeemed, saved, and possess the gift of eternal life (John 3:16). When I asked my dad why he and my mom got married after knowing each other for only three months, he said, "There was a very strong attraction between us, and it was our spiritual connection and faith in God that sealed the deal for us, and we agreed there was no reason to postpone our life together."

When I asked my mom the same question, she echoed what my dad said and added, "I would have followed your dad anywhere to be his wife and make a home for him and our children, because I knew he was following Jesus."

Born into a happy marriage, I was a happy child! Every early childhood memory gives me a strong sense of belonging, and I felt special. One of the main reasons for this was because my dad told me, from the earliest time I can remember, I was a Child of God, the Daughter of the King. Bubbling over with contentment and joy, every day was filled with love, affection, music, prayer, and a desire to create a life I loved, as my parents were doing.

My happiness was made complete when my little brother, Rusty, was born one month after I turned four. When my mom told me she was going to the hospital to bring back "your baby," I took her statement very seriously. Rusty captured my heart and my love at first glance. He had the sweetest little round face, big blue eyes, and deep dimples. He simply melted my heart into his. Though I was only four, I was constantly mindful of my baby brother, wanting to hold him, watching over him when he was asleep in his crib, changing his diapers or at least trying, feeding him, helping to bathe him, singing to him, and telling him how much I loved him.

My love for my brother was and always has been unconditional, and I have always affectionately called him "Bubby," an endearing nickname I have used throughout our lives. We were very close. In some ways we experienced some of the uncommon bond that twins experience; sensing when something was wrong, feeling what one of us might be feeling, understanding each other without words, and having no conflicts or misunderstandings between us. (Except when he took my clock radio apart to see how it worked and couldn't put it back together again.) We are bonded now and forevermore. He said I was more like a mom to him than a sister. He was the first boy I ever loved and was responsible for activating my mother's heart and my innate desire to nurture and protect.

God was at the helm and heart of our family. Being a Navy seaman, Dad often said, "God is the captain and commander of our ship." The soil of the heart and soul of our family was good, and it produced an abundant family garden. A Mississippi boy at heart, Dad was authentic. There was nothing hypocritical about him. He didn't "toot his own horn," as was the old saying from years gone by. He was humble. He knew who he was and didn't try to be anybody else. He was intelligent, athletic, and had a playful sense of humor and people often referred to him as a diamond in the rough.

Mom, meanwhile, portrayed all that was good about Southern women: warmth, charm, and hospitality. Everything was about her husband and making a home for us, their children. I once overheard a friend telling my mom that every piece of furniture in our home said, "Come in. Make yourself comfortable. You are welcome."

My brother and I enjoyed and benefitted from all that was good about our family life under God's protection and grace. It felt like we were living in a fairy tale.

With a vivid imagination since childhood, I have always been fascinated with stories about good triumphing over evil, always with a happy ending. While fairy tales do not deny the realities of evil, human frailty, and weaknesses, when good wins in the end, I celebrate! Such accounts about life, death, and the meaning of existence have always been what draws me into a book or movie.

I was 10 years old the day my dad and I sat on our front porch after a heavy rainstorm. The air was clean and fresh after dark clouds had hung overhead for three days, and the constant rain created a large and fairly deep puddle of water in a low part of the yard. As we sat on the porch, my dad reached down into a flower bed, picked up a small stone, and threw it into the water. "See the ripples the rock makes in the water when it falls to the bottom?" he asked. "That's what happens when we die. Though we are no longer alive here on earth, the ripples show us something of how we go on." He then asked, "Do you know where we go after we die?"

"Yes, Daddy. I know our body stays here and our spirit goes on to be with God in Heaven," I replied.

"Good," he said. "I'm glad to know you have eyes to

see and ears to hear." He added, "When I die, do not sit beside my grave. I will not be there. I will be living in eternity with God, face-to-face with Jesus, a citizen and resident of Heaven. Do not linger at my grave. Keep eternity in your heart. That's where I'll be."

"Okay, Daddy," I said, "But, I sure hope you live to be an old, white-haired man. I can't imagine my life without you."

I had no emotional reaction to what my dad shared about death, because I knew it was a teaching moment. Dad and I had many of these type of conversations. I considered him to be the wisest man on earth, wanting him to be the one who taught me about life and death too. As an adult, I've realized one of his many spiritual gifts was teaching. That afternoon was just another opportunity for him to share an important truth with me, so his words about death, and referring to when he might die, did not concern or frighten me.

Because I was living in what felt like a fairy tale, I was hopeful about the personal fairy tale I desired for my future—one where I'd grow up, get married, be a mother, and live happily ever after. I could have never imagined how much death, loss, and grief would become a significant part of my true-life story.

I was twelve and my brother was eight when my dad died of an undetected, undiagnosed massive heart attack on May 9, 1960. After church that morning, our family went to a close friend's house for a BBQ and pool party to celebrate Mother's Day. After several hours in the pool and sun, my dad told my mom he wasn't feeling well and we should probably go home. Rusty was still swimming. "Come on, Dad!" he called. "Get back in the pool with me. Let's play!" Dad got back in the water, and Rusty laughed, kept jumping on Dad's back, splashing water all over him.

A few minutes later, Dad got out of the pool, and I heard him tell my mom, "We need to say goodbye and get going now."

It seemed something was wrong, and he was in a hurry. When he told mom to drive, that seemed odd, he always drove us everywhere.

On the way home, we made a quick stop at the grocery store. Mom got out to pick up bread, bologna, and apples for our lunches. As we stayed in the car with Dad, Rusty and I noticed how Dad was leaning his head back on the passenger seat in front of us with his eyes closed.

"What's wrong?" I asked. "Do you have a headache?"

Rusty added, "Do you feel like you are going to throw up?"

In a weak voice, Dad replied, "I'm okay. I probably ate too much, and I'm tired from all the swimming I did today." My brother never forgot those words. Though he told no one, he would blame himself for Dad's death far into his adult years, because he thought he forced Dad to stay in the pool longer than he should have.

We arrived home, and Mom told us to get ready for bed as quickly and quietly as we could, so she could focus on getting Dad settled. Once we were both in our pajamas, had washed our faces and brushed our teeth, we ran into our parents' bedroom, jumped up on the bed with Dad, laid our heads on his chest, and said what we usually said every night, "I love you. Sleep tight, and don't let the bedbugs bite. See you in the morning." Because I knew Dad wasn't feeling well, I stayed a little longer, cuddling up and laying my head on his left shoulder with my left hand over his heart.

"I love you with all of my heart. I will ask God to make you feel better."

Dad smiled and put his right hand over mine. "That's my girl. Never stop believing in the faithfulness of God, staying close to Him no matter what happens in your life."

Kissing his cheek, I skipped off to bed with love in my heart and the hope and confidence that God would heal my dad.

After suffering silently—in the pool playing with Rusty, while we were driving home, waiting in the car for Mom to come out of the grocery store, and during the time Rusty and I were getting ready for bed—once he knew we were tucked in bed, he told Mom, "We need to go to the hospital now. Call JoAnn from next door to come over to be with the kids, and call Dave and Esther and ask them to meet us at the hospital. We have to go now."

A few hours later, he was dead.

It was about four A.M. when Esther, a close family friend I called "Mama Two," gently woke me from a deep, peaceful sleep.

"Honey, wake up. Your daddy is gone. He died of a heart attack last night."

Pulling the comforter up under my neck, I flipped over, burying my face in the pillow and screamed, "No! No! No! Not my dad! God, what have You done?"

I immediately blamed God for my dad's death because I believed, as I had been taught, He is the One with the power over life and death. Sobbing into my pillow, I started shaking all over, which I soon learned meant I was going into shock. Esther put her hands on my shoulders saying, "I'm so sorry, sweetie. I'm so sorry. Your daddy is in Heaven with God, and God will never leave you. He will be with you always."

At 12 years old, the idea that the Almighty, All-Powerful God of the universe would be with me always and would never leave me was comforting, but I was angry. When Esther left the room, I said out loud," Well, God. I guess You have to be my daddy now." Pushing my face deeper into the pillow I wept and said, "But, You are God, how are You going to take the place of my dad?"

For weeks and even months after my dad died, I had doubts about God. Why hadn't He healed my dad? He resurrected Jesus from the dead. I couldn't help but think maybe He wasn't such a loving and good God after all. Trusting Him and talking to Him in prayer wasn't as easy as before, and I always talked to Him before—I didn't want any misunderstandings between us.

As a family, we prayed together about everything with gratitude for our many blessings. My parents, grandparents, and other family members and friends declared their love for God all the time. We believed Jesus was God's Son, God with us, the Savior and Redeemer of the world. I had experienced the evidence of God as the Creator through nature, His love through my family, and at church. I couldn't remember not being aware of God's presence, even before acknowledging and accepting Jesus as my Savior, Lord, and King when I was eight.

Everything was right with my world—and then God took my dad when he was just 34 years old, making my 32-year-old mom a widow and Rusty and me fatherless.

With more questions than answers, what I thought I knew about God wasn't making sense. I was hurt, frustrated, and mad at Him.

Already deeply troubled, the first conversation with my mom the day after Dad died added to my distress. She was sitting in a chair sobbing with friends and family members gathered around her. She kept repeating, "The song is gone. The music is dead." She seemed inconsolable. It was all very confusing. *Why would she say the music is dead when she always told me God gives the song?* With Rusty's hand in mine, we stood in the doorway, and she motioned for us to come to her. Pulling me close, she said, "What are we going to do? You are going to have to help me."

How was I going to help her? I was 12 years old. If I had to help her, who was going to help me? My brother? Dad had always taken care of everything, and Mom was a homemaker who had never worked outside of our home. "God, if You are with me always, please be with my mom too," I prayed.

A few days later, standing over my dad's lifeless body in a casket, I knew he wasn't in that body anymore. There was no color in his face, no sign of life. He was gone, and I remembered him telling me to remember after he died he would be with God. In that very painful moment, I wanted to be with him and God too.

Stunned and feeling somewhat abandoned and left behind, I wondered what was to become of our family. We were incomplete. I was incomplete. Later that night, sitting alone in my bedroom and looking out the window at the moon and the countless stars, I felt like a tiny, insignificant speck in the universe.

One star twinkled brighter than all the rest—the North Star, which some biblical scholars think might be the star lighting the way to Heaven's gates. Trying to imagine Heaven and what my dad was doing in that moment, I wrote my first poem.

My Dad

My dad is in Heaven riding and racing on clouds.
Singing "Hallelujah!"
From his heart oh so loud!
He was a good man and a good dad.
When I think of him, I feel alone and sad.

In my mind and deep down in my heart
I believe one day with him on clouds I will ride.

I will kiss him and hug him, so happy I'll be.
And forever and ever he will be with me.

Days are hard.
Nights are long.
Mom says, "I've lost the music, my song."

At night, when I wake up and it's cold and dark,
I imagine my dad and God with me in the dark.

Then I feel much better and go back to sleep.
And, for a while, I do not weep.

Losing my dad was heartbreaking and turned my young life upside down and me inside out. I wasn't sure who I was anymore. Our home felt different. Mom was different. Because two of my dad's friends offered to divorce their wives and marry my mom, we left our church, which was hurtful and harmful for Rusty and me. Everything was different. We didn't know how to do life without my dad. There were countless times in the future when we not only missed, but needed him.

I missed him when he wasn't with me through my teen years, helping me with math. (I really needed his help with math.) When I was crowned homecoming princess in high school, I remember looking up in the football stadium seeing my mom and wishing my dad was sitting beside her. He would have been very proud of me when I won a gold medal for humorous interpretation at a community speech conference. Graduating from high school would have been a significant accomplishment, especially because we had talked about how he hoped I would go to college and earn a degree. I wonder what degree he imagined for me. It would have been import- ant to him to approve of the boys I dated, and when I fell in love and was married. He would have been a loving, attentive, and fun grandpa for my children.

To this very day, I miss my dad, and wonder if my life would have been different had he not died. The

1960s were challenging years for me because of my dad's death, the Vietnam War, and America's social and sexual revolution. Until then, my childhood was filled with dreams, fun and peace. My responsibilities were few because of my mom's superpowers of organization and homemaking. She required very little help from Rusty and me. Our primary focus was to trust and obey our parents who trusted and obeyed God. I was clueless about adult things.

Then, after a year of mourning, Mom had to go to work full-time. She tried very hard to create and maintain a sense of normalcy, but that was impossible with all the changes she was facing. She struggled to uphold the spiritual foundations she and my dad had created together for themselves and our family. Doing the best she could, she later had her fair share of regrets. The biggest was leaving the church we all loved, which negatively impacted the years that followed.

Though I kept God in my heart, I needed the covering, protection, guidance, and fellowship of being a part of a home church. We wandered from one church to another for a few years. Not only was my mom grieving the loss of her husband she was also very disappointed and disenchanted with those who called themselves Christians. No one seemed to really care about us. There were only a few close friends who walked with her through her grieving. It really hurt and angered her that not one man in the family or the church was willing to step in to be a supportive role model for Rusty.

As Bob Dylan wrote in his song, "The Times They Are a-Changin'" was true for us as a family as well as our nation. The changes were not good. I longed to go back to better days and better times.

Decades later, I would suffer an even greater loss and feel an even deeper overwhelming sorrow, and it seemed I might die of a broken heart.

CHAPTER TWO
A Preview

"The vision of the evenings and the mornings that has been told is true, but seal up the vision, for it refers to many days from now."
(Daniel 8:26, ESV)

OVER 40 YEARS AFTER MY DAD'S DEATH, and just two years before my youngest son, Kevin, died, I had a dream. Our family and a large group of friends were taking a cruise on a vintage clipper ship in a sea similar to the Mediterranean. The sky was clear and as brilliantly blue as the water beneath us. The ship's sails overhead mirrored the large, white, billowing clouds above in what felt like a dance of white. Warm, gentle breezes blew all around us. Wallowing in the beauty surrounding us was exhilarating.

Suddenly, out of nowhere, and with no warning, a monstrous storm brought torrential rains and towering waves pounding against the ship. Separated from everyone, I found myself alone in the lower level of the ship hunkered down in a corner. Never had I experienced such cold darkness. I felt abandoned and afraid. There was not so much as a glimmer of light anywhere when just seconds before I had been illuminated and warmed by the sun. Where were my husband, sons, family, and friends? Why was I alone in the dark?

Not strong enough to stay upright while being thrown around on the floor, I was nauseous, battered, sobbing, and I cried out to God, "Did You send this storm? Why are You doing this? Am I going to die?" The darkness and brutality I was experiencing seemed unending.

Beat up and helpless, finally a stream of faint morning light broke through the seams in the ship's planking. The abrupt, unsettling calm frightened me more than the storm itself. Breathless, confused, and exhausted, I clambered up the stairs to the main deck. It took a while to find my husband, Bob, standing with our sons, Eric and David. I was so glad to see them—but where was Kevin? I asked Bob, and he said he didn't know.

Fear gripped me. I urged my husband and sons to search for him.

The next scene in my dream was of Bob motioning for me to come to him. "Hon, come with me." He held out his hand and led me to a rope ladder we would use to climb down over the side of the ship to get in a rowboat. "What? I have to climb down that ladder into a rowboat? I can't do that; you know I'm afraid of heights. I'll freeze, lose my grip. I'll drown. Where are we going?"

Bob did not reply. He climbed down the ladder and called to me, "Come on, Hon. You can do this."

It took me quite a while to calm down and talk myself into gripping the rope, throwing my legs over the side of the ship, and climbing down the rope ladder, counting each step until Bob helped me into the rowboat. Thankfully, the sea was calm, or I wouldn't have even tried to climb down that ladder. Once I was seated in the boat, I asked Bob again, "Where are we going?"

With his hand on my arm, he said, "It's okay. Everything will be okay."

Eric and David rowed the boat through a shimmering, glassy sea, and no one spoke. The air was cool. The sky and clouds were reflected in the water. It felt like we were moving in slow motion. It all seemed surreal.

As we approached a sandy shore, I appreciated there were no waves, just the gentle ebb and flow of crystal-clear, turquoise water. Though the sun was warming, I was cold. I couldn't breathe. I couldn't think. I was afraid.

Once out of the boat, we all walked together toward two green, grassy knolls. As we got closer to the first mound, I could see the body of a young boy lying on top.

It was Kevin, as he looked when he was eight years old! My knees buckled, and I fell to the ground grieving the little boy I loved.

Then Bob helped me up and we walked toward the second knoll. As I drew closer, I could see the body of Kevin as a young adult, his current age. Screaming, I ran to my son, fell down over his body, pulled him close, holding him in my arms as I kept saying, "Not my boy. Not Kevin! Oh, God, what have You done now?!"

My screaming and weeping woke me up, and I realized I had been dreaming. Heart pounding, I got out of bed and down on my knees at the foot of my bed.

"God, why did I dream that dream?" I prayed. "Are You showing me something of things to come? Surely it is only a dream. Please, Lord, it has to be a dream! Please don't take my son."

After several moments on my knees, I stood up, took a deep breath, and said, "It will be okay. It has to be okay!" The entire time I was getting ready to go to work, I kept talking to God, pleading with Him, "Please, I can't lose Kevin. Am I going to lose Kevin? I can't lose Kevin!"

I needed to talk to Bob, but we didn't have cell

phones then, and he was on duty as an air traffic controller at Long Beach Airport and wasn't supposed to
a receive phone calls unless it was because of an emergency. Also, knowing him the way I did, he would have
probably thought I was being hysterical over a dream,
and he would have been irritated with me for calling.

When I got to work, I immediately met with my boss,
Michael, and our coworker, Stella. Both were special friends
and spiritual mentors. After sharing the dream, Michael
said, "Let's pray. Perhaps Kevin's mortal life is in danger."

We all hoped it was just a dream.

When I later told Bob, he said, "It was just a dream.
It was just a bad dream."

Two years later, a large crowd of family and friends
would gather at the edge of Kevin's green, grassy grave
under bright blue skies and billowing white clouds.

A few weeks after Kevin died, I told Eric, David, and the
rest of our family about the dream I had two years earlier.
Our daughter-in-law, Vel, then revealed she had dreamed
that Kevin died about the same time I had my dream. For
reasons known only to God, He foretold Kevin's death to
us, just as He had revealed the death of Jesus to His mother,
Mary, through the prophet Simeon (Luke 2:28–35).

Webster's Dictionary defines a revelation as "the divine
or supernatural disclosure to humans of a surprising and

previously unknown fact—the unfolding, uncovering, or bringing to light of something that was previously secret." Dreams recorded in Scripture serve a purpose established by God. They have been given by the Father and recorded by His children for the sake of the Church, the body of believers in God, throughout time.

In her article on the Christianity.com website, writer Candice Lucey said, "Every prophecy, direction, or warning is relevant to Christians today." She also wrote, "A dream is something you are aware of at some level. It might be fragmentary, disconnected, and illogical, but if you aren't aware of it during sleep then it isn't a dream . . . The Scripture declares the influence of the Spirit of God upon the soul extends to its sleeping as well as its waking thoughts."

Whatever God's purpose is concerning visions and dreams, Vel and I are grateful He shared His "supernatural disclosure" about Kevin with us. We are both sensitive, emotional, and passionate women, and at that time there were several toddlers and young children in our family. Had we not been given our dreams, the shock of Kevin's sudden death could have been too much for us to handle while carrying out our responsibilities as wives and mothers. We thank God for trusting and preparing us for what was to come.

CHAPTER THREE

One More Look at You

"We look not to things that are seen but to the things that are unseen. For the things that are seen are transient, but the things that are unseen are eternal."

(2 Corinthians 4:18, ESV)

NESTLED UNDER THE COVERS ON A COLD JANUARY morning, I hit the snooze alarm several times before waking to the clapping of flip-flops. Opening my sleepy eyes, I was very happy to see Kevin walking into the room. No longer living at home, he often stopped by on his way to or from someplace or to pick up something. Bob and I were glad he hadn't moved all of his clothes and personal belongings from the house. We looked forward to the snippets of time when we could visit and connect with him again.

We were not enjoying our empty nest. We missed our boys who were now men. Eric and David were married with children, and Kevin was engaged to be married in June, but he still had most of his personal belongings in our home so he routinely stopped by. Unlike Eric and David, Kevin wasn't in a hurry to grow up and leave home. He was young at heart and acted boyish at times. His Uncle Rod referred to him as a "man child," likening him to the fictitious character, Peter Pan, who never wanted to grow up. Yet soon after he met the love of his life, Venus (Vee), our Peter Pan decided to step into manhood.

At 26, he was the youngest manager hired by the Black Angus Steakhouse restaurant chain. He worked hard and was very successful in the restaurant business. With the personality and skillset for serving, pleasing, and working well with others, he created and maintained a positive, cohesive dining environment and staff. Family members, neighbors, and friends often went to the restaurant to eat and watch him and his team in action. The restaurant and bar were always filled to capacity with those Kevin called "regulars." Anyone who knew him said he was the reason they came to the restaurant. He had charisma and knew how to make everyone feel important, welcome, and accepted.

He and his brother, David, had plans to open their own restaurant one day. David had earned his culinary arts degree from the Le Cordon Bleu College of Culinary Arts in Pasadena, California. With them working side by side, the restaurant would have been very successful, and I was looking forward to working for them part-time. We were all very excited about the future.

At what would turn out to be our last family Christmas gathering in 2001, Kevin looked tired, pale, and his face seemed puffy, even bloated. When I asked if he was eating and sleeping well, he said, "Not really, Mom. There's a lot going on." I moved closer to him. "Son, you are giving yourself away and burning the candle at both ends. Please take better care of yourself. I'm concerned about you."

He smiled, gently hugged me, and patted me on the shoulder as he had done since he was a toddler. "No one takes better care of me than you, Mom, but don't worry about me. I'm okay."

Weeks later, the sound of his flip-flops and the fragrance of Giò cologne announced his warming presence in my room. The sight of him with his hat turned backward, wearing his long-sleeved Katin T-shirt and surf trunks made me smile. I was really glad to see him. My sons have always been eye candy. Just to look at them delights me as a mother.

As Kevin slowly and quietly moved toward the foot of the bed, I said, "Hey, snuggle worm, what's up?" Ever since he was old enough to climb in and out of his crib, Kevin had snuck into our room in the middle of the night to wriggle his way under the covers, earning him that nickname. More often than not, Bob and I didn't know he was in bed with us until we woke up to find him asleep between us or lying on his back with his arms behind his head smiling and obviously very pleased with himself. When he was eight, Bob asked him why he kept coming into our bed at night. "I get cold, and I like to cuddle." He also said he knew we liked it when he slept with us. We did. No one liked to cuddle and get cozy like Kevin.

Pulling the comforter up around my neck, I sat up. "What's up?" I asked once more. "Where are you headed?"

Kevin replied softly, "Hey, Mom. There's a storm up north bringing fifteen- to sixteen-foot swells to Dog Patch. Todd and I are heading down to surf." Dog Patch is a pristine beach in San Onofre, California, where locals have surfed for decades. Kevin called it his "sweet spot." When he was in his early twenties, he bought a framed picture of Dog Patch for his room. After hanging it up, he called his dad and me into his room to show us the picture. "When I die, that's where I want to meet Jesus."

Though Kevin was a strong swimmer and an avid surfer who had surfed in big waves and cold water many times before, that morning I was concerned. I had never been concerned about Bob or any of the boys surfing. Thinking of him paddling out in freezing cold water while being pounded by powerful waves, I almost told him to be careful, but a still, quiet voice inside me said, "Don't send him off that way." Instead, I said, "Cowabunga, dude!"

Kevin giggled. "Okay, Mom."

Patting the head of our little dog, Nikki, who lay asleep at the foot of the bed, he glanced around the room, looked at me, and grinned. I remember it was his emerald-green eyes that caught my attention. His eyes were the mirrors of his soul, filled with warmth and love. We locked eyes. *He is so beautiful, so handsome. I love him so much,* I thought as he turned and walked out of the room as quietly and slowly as he had entered it.

Suddenly, I was cold. Shivering, I lay down and listened to the hum of the engine of his truck. I didn't recall ever doing that before. It seemed as though Kevin was staying in the driveway much longer than normal. Usually, he turned the key and off he went. I wondered what he might be doing. Maybe he was on his cell phone calling Todd to say he was on his way. Perhaps he was making sure he had everything he needed: wetsuit, booties, and towel. It could be he was securing his surfboard in the back of the truck.

How I wish I had gotten up and gone outside to see what he was doing.

At least then I could have had one last look at him. One last hug. One last goodbye.

Weeks after Kevin died, Bob and I learned he had stopped by David's house the night before to visit and talk about how things were going in their lives. David said the conversation quickly went deep with each sharing what was right and good, and what might need changing. They also laughed a lot.

We also learned before leaving Venus to go surfing the morning he died, Kevin told her he was exhausted and didn't really want to go surfing, but he didn't want to let Todd down. Venus encouraged him to stay home and rest. When her mom, Jan, said goodbye to him, as he was leaving the house, she noticed Kevin had a faraway look in his eyes. That unnerved her. She felt she might not see him again, and she wondered why she would think such a horrible thought

Before coming to our house that morning, he had stopped by his brother Eric's house to ask him to go surfing with him. During their visit, Kevin told his 12-year-old niece, Nicole, she was beautiful. And, he wanted hugs from Eric, Nicole, and Eric's son, Joey.

There are no words to express my gratitude to God that Kevin stopped by our house next, and I was home rather than at work. To this day, I still have questions about that morning. Was he happy to see my car in the driveway? What went through his mind as he opened the courtyard gate, walked up the sidewalk to the front door coming home? What was he feeling physically and emotionally? Did he have a sense that day was different somehow?

Those final moments with my precious son remind me to never take those I love for granted. From that day on, I have always said, "I love you" at all partings and goodbyes.

CHAPTER FOUR

Into the Shadows

"Though I walk through the valley of the shadow of death, I will fear no evil; For You are with me; Your rod and Your staff, they comfort me."

(Psalm 23, NKJV)

AFTER KEVIN DROVE OUT OF THE DRIVEWAY that morning, I stayed in bed thinking about how much he meant to me. Time passed, and I soon realized I was going to be late for work. Once dressed and ready to leave the house, I hurried toward the front door when a loud, high-pitched beeping like a smoke alarm started going off. Turning away from the door, I realized the sound was coming from the telephone in the kitchen. It had never made that noise before. When I picked up the receiver, I listened to a voice-mail from a nurse at San Clemente Hospital.

"This is an emergency. Please call the following number immediately."

My hands were shaking as I punched in the number connecting me to the emergency department. "I just received a call from this number. My name is Angie Green."

"Are you Kevin Green's mother?"

"Yes, I am."

"Mrs. Green, we have your son at the emergency room. He's been in a critical surfing accident."

"A critical surfing accident?" I repeated.

"Yes, Mrs. Green. Do you have someone who can come with you to the hospital?"

"Yes, I will call my husband, and we will be there as soon as we can."

The phone slipped out of my hand and crashed onto the kitchen counter. It startled me. I jumped. As I picked up the phone to hang it up, my hands were shaking. My entire body was trembling, and I remembered that happening when I was told my dad had died. I was going into shock. It felt as though my heart was being crushed in a vice, and it was beating very hard and fast. I felt dizzy and sick to my stomach. My mind was reeling. I knew Kevin was not in critical condition. He was gone.

As I paced aimlessly around the island in the kitchen, I cried out to God, "No. No. No! You took my dad. Why are You taking my son?" Fear and panic gripped me, and I instantly recalled the dream from two years earlier. It wasn't just a dream after all. It foretold what was to come. Struggling to breathe, time stood still. I was paralyzed with fear and don't remember calling Bob.

Eric drove Bob and me to the hospital. On the way, Kevin's friend, Todd, called Eric on his cell. Eric held the phone away from his ear so Bob and I could hear what Todd was saying. With a gentle, sad voice, he told Eric, "Kevin's gone, bro! The paddle out was brutal. When we finally made it out to calmer water, I had a hard time catching my breath. Sitting up on my board, I heard a splash, thinking Kevin was in the water diving for sea turtles or playing around, as he usually does. Breathing heavily, I looked his way and saw he was face down in the water. I swam over to him, got him on his board, and turned him over to start CPR, but he was gone. I wanted to save him, Eric. I think he died as soon as he sat up on his board."

Until that call, Eric had been driving as fast as he could. Now he slowed down. There was no longer any urgency to get there. Burying my face in my hands and covering my mouth to muzzle my weeping and wailing, I unfastened the seatbelt, got down on my knees in the backseat, with my face in the seat and screamed. "No. No. No! Not my baby boy! Not our Kevin!"

Bob refused to believe it. "This can't be true. This can't be happening," he kept saying.

"It's true, Dad," Eric confirmed. "Kevin is gone."

This can't be real, I thought.

When we arrived at the hospital, a nurse led us to the room where Kevin's lifeless body lay. He looked as though he was sleeping peacefully with a slight smile on his beautiful face. Stepping close to him on one side of the gurney with Bob on the other, I ran my fingers through Kevin's wet and sandy hair. Looking down, I noticed he was lightly covered in sand from head to foot. His flip-flops were on his feet, and there were little bits of sand and grit between his toes. With my face against his, I kissed him and tasted the saltwater on his cheek. Because Bob and the boys were surfers, I had enjoyed a thousand salty kisses and cleaned up after sandy feet many times. Years later, I'd find a sign that still hangs in our home with the words "sandy toes and salty kisses" etched into the wood. It constantly reminds me of that moment in the hospital, and it always takes my breath away.

Moving to the foot of the gurney to allow his brothers, his fiancée Venus, and the rest of the family to move closer to Kevin, the sight of them standing over him, holding his hands, touching him, and patting his head while they wept ripped my heart apart. I had to leave the room. Standing in the hallway, I put my hands over my ears to shut out the sounds of sorrow. Death was all around me, and I was reminded of the dream of me by myself in the dark in the lower deck of the ship in a monstrous storm. I was living the dream, and life as I knew it was being swept away. *This can't be real,* I thought. Sharp pains shot through my heart. I was overwhelmed with grief.

A few minutes later, the ER doctor approached me, and I called for Bob to join us in the hall. I have no idea what the doctor looked like, his name, or how he greeted us. All I remember is he asked us a lot of questions about Kevin's health and medical history. That conversation is a blur until he told us, because Kevin had died in a public place, his body would have to be taken to the county coroner's office for an autopsy to determine the cause of death.

The idea of an autopsy being performed on our son deeply troubled Bob and me. My mind shot to an image from a movie I saw of a young man dead and laid out on a metal table in a morgue. That image horrified me. *How could this be happening? Why is this happening?*

When the emergency medical technicians came to move Kevin's body, everyone followed behind the gurney through the halls to the transport vehicle. We watched as the gurney was lifted into the back and the doors were closed. Pulling my arms into my chest and over my heart, I had never felt so injured, wounded, and broken.

Every part of me screamed, "No. No. No!" I could feel death. I could taste it.

Leaving the hospital without our son was devastating. I do not remember anything about the drive home. Once there, though, Bob and I were glad to see the loving faces of many of our family and friends. Weeping filled our home. It was as if a tidal wave of grief rolled in and over us. My greatest fear had always been of drowning in a tidal wave. That day, I was drowning in a sea of sorrow.

It wasn't until about two A.M. when Bob and I decided we would try to get some sleep. Before getting into bed, I went into Kevin's room and started searching through drawers, looking for something of his to wear or hold. Folded neatly in the bottom drawer of his dresser were the Superman beanie and T-shirt he wore when he was a boy. Cradling them in my arms, as if I was holding Kevin, I fell face down on his bed, sobbing uncontrollably into his pillow. Comforted by the scent of him on his pillow, I wondered how long that scent would remain, and I thought I would never wash it again. Once in bed, Bob and I talked about the horror of the day. We fell asleep in each other's arms with Kevin's beanie and T-shirt between us. Despite the warmth of the covers over us and the closeness of our bodies, never had I been so cold.

Several years after Kevin died, Bob told me he often went into Kevin's bedroom leaning into the closet to breathe in the scent of him. Kevin left a sweet fragrance behind in so many ways.

The next morning, my first thought and the words I spoke were, "Kevin is dead!" Pulling the comforter over my head and flipping over into my pillow, I sobbed fresh tears and again thought of doing the very same thing long ago when I was told my dad was dead.

Bob was up, and there was the smell of fresh coffee brewing and familiar voices coming from the family room. Making myself get out of bed, I quietly closed the bedroom door, knelt down, and prayed. Though still in shock, I was surprised at how the words of my pain and sorrow flowed so easily. "God, please help us do what we have to do for the love of our son. Give us Your strength in our weakness. Draw us close to You, knowing You will keep Your promise to draw close to us in our brokenness. Your love and grace is sufficient, because Your power is made perfect in our weakness."

At the end of my prayer, I reached for my Bible as if it was a lifeline. Sitting on the floor with my back against the foot of the bed, I frantically searched for words of comfort and hope. This was what I found and recorded that morning: *"Fear not, for I am with you; be not dismayed, for I am your*

God; I will strengthen you, I will help you, I will uphold you with my righteous right hand" (Isaiah 41:10, ESV). "*The LORD is my strength and my song, and he has become my salvation; this is my God, and I will praise Him, my father's God, and I will exalt Him*" (Exodus 15:2, ESV). "*Behold, God is my salvation; I will trust, and will not be afraid; for the LORD GOD is my strength and my song, and He has become my salvation*" (Isaiah 12:2, ESV). "*For God gave us a spirit not of fear but of power and love and self-control*" (2 Timothy 1:7, ESV).

Holding the Bible to my heart, I thought about the words from Ephesians 6:17 telling us how the sword of the Spirit is the Word of God. Thanking God for my "sword," I stood up, took a deep breath, got dressed, and joined my family. My hope and strength were renewed!

That day our lifelong friends, Sharon and Tony, arrived from Northern California and stayed with us for the next week. Having them with us around the clock comforted and strengthened us, as did the outpouring of sympathy, love, and concern from family, friends, neighbors, church members, and coworkers. At times, the phone calls, flower and food deliveries, and visits were draining. The day before the graveside and memorial services, we had to let phone calls go to voicemail, and we posted a sign on the front gate letting people know we needed time to rest. Everyone was exhausted.

After learning what I have about grief, we didn't

know we could have buried Kevin's body then and had a memorial service to celebrate his life at a later time. We never thought of doing something like that, especially because family and friends came from out of town and some from out of state. Though it was difficult, with God's presence and the help of family and friends, we did what we felt we had to do.

We decided to bury Kevin at the Forest Lawn cemetery close to our house. Finding a place to lay Kevin's body to rest was a heart-wrenching experience—another awful reminder of the reality of death. After meeting with a salesperson, she took us to a plot at the base of a beautiful marble statue of Jesus with children gathered around Him. To the right of Jesus were three little boys standing close together facing Him.

The older of the three, dressed as a shepherd, stood behind the two younger boys with his arms on their shoulders. That figure actually looked like our oldest son, Eric, when he was a boy. The next oldest boy had his right arm up in front of his face depicting his timidity and shyness. He resembled our son, David. The youngest boy's arms were stretched out in front of him with a look on his face that said, "Let's go!" That figure looked like Kevin, always ready for an adventure, meeting someone new, or doing something different. As we gazed at the three boys reaching toward the sculpture of Jesus, Bob and I knew that was the place we would bury Kevin. We believed that plot was meant for our son.

In that painful moment, I took my first step into the shadows of death as a big, black cloud passed overhead in the sky, quickly followed by the brightness of the sun. After my dad died, I learned how the valley of the shadows of death could be a dark and lonely place with some wild parts—parts where someone could lose their way and get lost. Bereavement professionals often refer to grief as an unchartered territory, a wilderness, a desert. For me, grieving was a walk, a journey, and I knew I needed God, and those willing to walk with me, through the valley. There were a few times after I started my journey through the shadows when I could have gotten lost. I certainly paused and stumbled a lot. It would have been very helpful to know at the beginning of my walk that the fear of losing my way and faltering was normal.

In my darkest times, I was introduced to the writings of Pierre Teilhard de Chardin, SJ, which encouraged me to give myself permission to grieve with patience and trust in God. Teilhard de Chardin was a French Jesuit priest, scientist, paleontologist, theologian, and philosopher who lived from May 1881 to April 1955. Not necessarily agreeing with all of his ideas and philosophies, particularly his belief in Darwin's theory of evolution, the words of his writings such as this one spoke wisdom and truth into my grieving.

Patient Trust

Above all, trust in the slow work of God.
We are quite naturally impatient in everything to
reach the end without delay.
We should like to skip the intermediate stages.
We are impatient of being on the way to something
unknown, something new.

And yet it is the law of all progress
that it is made by passing through some stages of
instability—
and that it may take a very long time.

And so, I think it is with you;
your ideas mature gradually—let them grow,
let them shape themselves, without undue haste.

Don't try to force them on,
as though you could be today what time
(that is to say, grace and circumstances acting on
your own good will)
will make of you tomorrow.

Only God could say what this new spirit
gradually forming within you will be.
Give Our Lord the benefit of believing
that his hand is leading you, and accept the anxiety
of feeling
yourself in suspense and incomplete.

　—Pierre Teilhard de Chardin, SJ, *Hearts on Fire*

Putting my hope and trust in God, I accepted "the anxiety of feeling (myself) in suspense and incomplete." No longer in shock, with a clear head and emotions less raw, I imagined myself at the edge of the valley of the shadows with Jesus at my side. Positioning myself as a sheep in His pasture, I decided to stay close to Him. Aware of His presence, I listened for His voice to lead and guide me, for him to protect and encourage me to not wander away from Him, go astray, and end up in danger. My grief was as ferocious as a lion, and I could have easily been devoured if I had not stayed close to the Good Shepherd.

"Know that the LORD is God. It is He who made us, and we are His; we are His people, the sheep of His pasture."
(Psalm 100:3, ESV)

"My sheep hear my voice, and I know them, and they follow me. I give them eternal life, and they will never perish, and no one will snatch them out of my hand."
(John 10:27–28, ESV)

CHAPTER FIVE

At the Edge of the Grave

"There is a time for everything, and a season for every activity under the heavens. A time to live and a time to die."

(Ecclesiastes 3:1, NIV)

IT DOESN'T SEEM THE NATURAL ORDER OF THINGS for a child to die before a parent, but it happens more often throughout the world than we might know. A 2022 "Our World in Data" summary indicates more than 15,000 children die every day—statistics for infant and child mortality. These numbers do not include teens or young adults so the number would be much higher. In centuries past, the death rate for infants and children was much higher, but I had no idea we are still losing babies, children, teens, and young adults at such a rate.

To suffer the loss of a child at any age for any cause is an unthinkable tragedy, and there are many decisions that must be made. As we planned a graveside and memorial service, we were faced with the expenses of laying our son's body to rest. Grief was intensified by the pressure of time and the high price tag attached to our plans. It seemed to us then and now, that the high costs of burial add insult to injury, and we don't understand why life savings must be spent to offset the expenses of burials.

Because of the loving generosity of my great-uncle, Faye, who owned Pettigrew & Sons Casket Company in Sacramento, California, Kevin's body would lay in a beautiful silver casket (if one thinks of a casket as beautiful).

A gift from my uncle and his family, he and his wife, Althea, drove the casket down from Sacramento in the back of their station wagon and delivered it to the Forest Lawn Mortuary in Cypress. What a blessing they were to us in our greatest time of need. We will never forget their example of extravagant love and grace.

When Kevin's body was delivered to the Forest Lawn Mortuary, Kevin's fiancée Venus, and two of her and Kevin's close friends had been given permission to prepare his body for viewing and subsequent burial; their friend, Alexis, was a certified mortician cosmetologist. Venus invited me to join them, but I couldn't, and that was the right decision for me. Cherishing memories when he was a boy of bathing, dressing, and combing his hair were the memories I wanted to remember not those of washing and dressing his lifeless, autopsied body. Those three young women expressed their courageous love for Kevin, and our family honors and loves them deeply for doing what we couldn't do. Knowing it was them, rather than a stranger, who prepared Kevin's body was of great comfort to all of us. We are forever grateful to them for their extravagant love.

Connected emotionally by our Irish/Scottish DNA, roots, and heritage, it was important for us to follow the cultural tradition of hosting a viewing in our home before closing and locking the casket for burial. To say a final goodbye, and to have one last look at our son with family and friends was very important to us. Wakes and viewings have been a significant death ritual in many cultures throughout the world for centuries. It seemed the right thing for us to do. We didn't want family and friends viewing Kevin's body at a mortuary. We wanted his body to be at home.

Some people were surprised, and a bit unnerved, that we brought Kevin's body home, positioning the casket in the dining room. Though an emotional and painful evening, being in the company of others who loved Kevin was comforting and meaningful. With a full house of more than a hundred people coming and going, there were times I wanted to hide. There were so many people to greet, all pulling me close or leaning into me to share words of love and sympathy. Yet to this day, I cannot recall anything anyone said other than, "I'm sorry."

The exception was Elmer, a childhood friend of our family, a big Samoan, who wrapped his arms around me. Pressing down on me as he shook and wept, I almost fell under his weight. What hurt the most was hearing him repeat, "Oh, Mama, we've lost our Kevin. Oh, Mama, we've lost our Kevin."

Love and grief filled the spaces where there had always been lively conversations, celebrations, and the laughter of a passionate and playful family. Hearing people talk about what Kevin meant to them was especially comforting and lifted my spirits. Just hearing his name spoken was a blessing, but it also was the constant reminder he was gone. At one point, I stood over the casket with my friend, Cecile, "We've got to get our boy in the ground," I told her. "It's been four days, and he's starting to smell bad." Though a raw reality, it confirmed Kevin was no longer in the body where his soul and spirit had once dwelled. The essence and substance of him was gone. It was time to bury his lifeless, decaying body.

After everyone left, Bob and I were alone with the

task of closing and locking the casket. Covering Kevin's body with his great-grandmother's quilt, we looked at some of the things people had placed in the casket: notes, flowers, a Hawaiian lei. The objects reminded me of when our son, Eric, had placed a baseball in his great-grandad's casket in remembrance of his love of the game. I giggled as I recalled hearing the sound of the baseball rolling around inside the casket as it was being carried to the grave. Some might find that odd, but for some reason we Irish are known for our sense of humor and comic relief in times of trouble. That funny memory provided much-needed grief relief in an intensely painful moment. It was just what I needed.

My husband and I stood over our son's body for quite a while and wept. He then said, "It's time. Honey, it's time." Knowing it was the last time we would see our son's beautiful face, I shivered, and Bob hung his head. Laying our hands gently on Kevin's chest, Bob patted the top of his head. I kissed his cheek. It was so cold, no warmth at all. He had always been our "warming fire." Bob kissed his forehead and said, "I love you, buddy," before we both said, "Goodnight, son."

As one, we shut the casket lid and Bob locked it. In that moment, just like on the island in my dream, I grieved my baby, my boy, and the young man that Kevin had become. Memories of Bob and me tucking him in bed, holding him, kissing him, and telling him we loved him played in my mind like scenes in a movie. Resting our hands on the top of the casket, we prayed the prayer we had spoken over our sons throughout their childhoods. "Now I lay me down to sleep. I pray the Lord my soul to keep. If I should die before I wake, I pray the Lord my soul to take." Kevin would not wake up. God had taken his soul.

The next morning, we woke to the sounds of family and friends talking quietly, making breakfast, and tidying up the house. They were familiar, welcome sounds to start a day that was going to be very busy in preparation to bury our son. It seemed once more everything was being done in slow motion.

It was midmorning when the hearse pulled up in front of our house to transport our son's body to the cemetery for the graveside service. As the attendants began to move the casket toward the front door, I couldn't watch. Turning away, I walked through the house calling to the women, "Please come and pray with me." In a circle holding hands, my friend, Barbara, asked God to be with us and to calm and strengthen us. At the close of the prayer, I said, "I don't think I can do this." That was instantly followed with a reminder from that place where God's Word is hidden in my heart, and I said, *"But, I can do all things through Christ who strengthens me. His strength will be my strength"* (Philippians 4:13, NKJV).

Bob and I drove to the cemetery in silence. Grief and anxiety gripped me like it had on the days each of our sons were born. As I had dreaded the labor pains of birthing them, I wanted to turn back and not go through what I knew was going to be a very painful process ahead. In what seemed an impossible situation to bear, the words of Matthew 19:26 NIV comforted and encouraged me: *"With man this is impossible, but with God all things are possible."*

Taking several deep breaths, the melody and lyrics of Amy Grant's song "Breath of Heaven (Mary's Song)" penetrated my heart, holding me together and bringing light to my darkness as God's holiness poured over me. The lyrics of the song I could remember ministered comfort and hope. I was strengthened knowing the very breath of Heaven filled my lungs and was all around me.

When we arrived at the grave site, the funeral director and his attendants removed the casket from the back of the hearse. This time I watched. It hurt so much, but I kept my eyes on the men who had agreed to be the pallbearers. As they all gathered around the casket, they gently carried it up the steps leading to the long sidewalk that led to the open grave. Our plan was for the men in the family to bear the burden of the casket to the grave while the women followed carrying flowers. It was symbolic to have the sobering task of burial accompanied by a measure of beauty.

Bob, Venus, and I led the procession of family and friends following behind the casket. As we walked, I grieved not only for the loss of our son but also for Venus, who would have been our daughter-in-law. We loved her and knew how much she and Kevin loved each other. In that moment, I was more concerned about her than myself.

A Scottish bagpiper wearing the Black Watch tartan colors (dark blue, medium green, light green, and black) and kilt of Bob's family clan led the long line of our procession to the grave. Two of my cousins wearing the Stewart colors of our Pettigrew clan followed, providing a sense of guardianship over the people walking ahead of them. There was a large crowd of people standing on all sides of the grave, forming a very large circle. The funeral director told us later it was the largest crowd at a graveside service he had ever seen in his 30-year career.

When our family was seated, I heard a woman standing somewhere behind me say, "It's as though they are burying a prince. This feels like a royal funeral." As far as we are concerned, we are a royal family, not of earthly blood, but the royal blood of Jesus, the King of Kings, Lord of LORDS. The blood of the Son of the most high God runs through our veins, for we are heirs to the Kingdom of God (Romans 8:17). Kevin was our prince, as are Eric and Dave.

Our son, Eric, and a dear friend and pastor, Bill Ward, welcomed everyone and opened our time together with tender words about Kevin and that our comfort and hope is in Christ. In those moments, an indescribable sense of peace warmed me followed by an epiphany: Jesus was present. Looking around the crowd, I knew He was there as *"a very present help"* in our time of trouble (Psalm 46:1, KJV). I also felt God was holding and covering me as He tells us He does in Psalm 91:4, KJV. *"He shall cover you with His feathers / And under His wings you shall take refuge."* Sixteen years later, my precious brother, Russ, was dying of cancer. The day before he died, he told me, "Sis, last night God held me through the night. I have never felt so loved, safe, and at peace."

After loving, encouraging words were spoken by our family, we invited everyone to pass by the casket laying their flowers on top. Most people paused to say their final goodbye. Some left their flowers and hurried past. It was obviously too painful for them. When the last person passed by the casket, I moved to stand next to Bob. The funeral director stepped forward and began to lower the casket into the ground. As so often throughout that dreadful week, I couldn't breathe. My heart started pounding hard and fast. I wanted to scream, "NO! STOP! NOT YET!"

Squeezing Bob's hand with what he later told me felt like a death grip, I said nothing—but cringed with each and every grinding turn of the handle as the device lowered my son's casket into the deep and empty hole in the ground. Sounds of weeping and gasps from the crowd of people expressed my emotions, as I faced what I dreaded most. This was it. Kevin's life was finished. Stepping to the edge of the grave, I dropped the flowers I was holding one by one, watching them land on top of the casket. Lowering my head, I whispered, "I hate death. We are not meant to die." The passage leaped to mind, *"For the wages of sin is death, but the free gift of God is eternal life in Christ Jesus our Lord"* (Romans 6:23, ESV).

Once the casket was settled, I shuddered. Bob and I picked up a handful of dirt and dropped it into the grave, as did others in our family. For us, the ritual echoed the phrase, "ashes to ashes, dust to dust," and symbolized how Kevin's body would return to dust. Bob told me years later, as he read this chapter, I actually threw the dirt and looked angry. I do not remember doing that, but I know it was how I felt. I also felt like I was covered in ashes. Yet, in that darkest moment of my life, I had a strong, defiant sense of victory over death, and the words from an old hymn, "Victory in Jesus," came to my mind. This song assured me Jesus had sought and bought Kevin, and He was my son's victory over death.

The last to stand at the edge of Kevin's grave were my mom and our dear friend, Tony, who called out to me and held up the to-do list he had been responsible for in preparing for this day. Ripping it in half, he dropped it into the open grave. "Look, Ang," he said. "It's done. It's finished!"

My mother stepped toward me, put her arms around me, and said, "My prayer for you is you will have a holy grief." I believed those words were spoken through her by the Holy Spirit. But, I asked myself, *What is a holy grief?*

Over time, it became clear that God was telling me to protect, guard, and preserve the sacred space in my soul created by and for Him.

Grief

Why do we race from pain when we can learn
Life's greatest lessons wrapped in grief and tears?
When sheltered from the flames so fierce which burn,
We huddle in despair, trapped in our fears.

A jewel lies hidden deep within such pain
Awaiting bravery to win the fight.
Its colors glow of wisdom to be gained
With patience and endurance gleaming bright.

So grasp the hand of misery and pain,
And breathe in strength and courage to belong.
Embrace the arms of sadness that remain,
And warble in the language of a song.
For pain becomes our friend in life indeed.
Its barrenness transforms and sets us free.

—Lana Gray, *The Truth That Can't Be Told 2*

CHAPTER SIX

In Remembrance of You

"Place me like a seal over your heart, like a seal on your arm; for love is as strong as death."

(Song of Solomon 8:6, NIV)

A MEMORIAL SERVICE IMMEDIATELY FOLLOWED the graveside service at the church we called home when our boys were young. It began with our sons, Eric and David, and Kevin's fiancée Venus, carrying Kevin's longboard down the center aisle and laying it on the communion table. This was done to signify our surrendering and releasing him to God, affirming our belief that it is the LORD who gives and takes away.

The church was filled to capacity with hundreds of people. As I looked around the sanctuary, there were faces familiar and unfamiliar. Bob and I had no idea Kevin's community was so large, but it didn't surprise us. Everyone Kevin was close to thought they were his best friend. He was certainly theirs.

A family friend and pastor, Charlie, officiated the service. Eric and David went forward to share about their brother, but only Eric could speak. David held his hand over his face trying to hold back his tears. It reminded me of the marble figure of the little boy that looked like him at the head of Kevin's grave. Eric paraphrased the words of Ecclesiastes 3:1–2 as he spoke. "There is a time for everything under Heaven, a time to live and a time to die." He added, "The tragedy is not that Kevin died; we all will die. The tragedy would have been if he was never born at all." Seeing my sons broken and grieving was a terrible tragedy.

Bob and I went forward next to share a few words and to add Kevin's name to the Births and Deaths page of our family Bible—our way of giving him his right of passage. Watching Bob pen Kevin's name and the date he died on the page brought a sense of closure I didn't expect. This was the first time in days I took in a deep breath of air. As the air filled my lungs, I imagined it to be a breath of Heaven I gladly received.

The entire service was filled with love, beauty, and laughter as several people shared what Kevin meant to them. The common themes were how Kevin was beautiful, loving, gentle, loyal, playful, silly, wise, fun, and funny, and how he made everyone happy just being in his presence. Hearing all of the expressions of love was comforting but painful because I knew it would be all those things and more I would miss about him. Kevin was leaving a very big hole in everyone's hearts. I asked, *Will the hole in my heart be there for the rest of my life? Could anything ever fill that huge, gaping hole? Do I want anything to fill it?*

After the service, we gathered in the fellowship hall at the church where the women's hospitality committee served a pasta buffet provided by Spaghettini in Seal Beach. David was the manager of its affiliate, Cucina Deli in Long Beach. The meal was delicious, and the spirit within the packed room of people who loved Kevin and our family warmed me all over. Sounds of lively conversations and laughter felt normal. *Surely, this is a taste of Heaven*, I thought, and I imagined Kevin repeating, as he often had, what Tiny Tim says in Charles Dickens's book *A Christmas Carol*—"God bless us every one!" Though I was in distress, I felt blessed in that sacred time and place.

Bob and I took quite a while saying goodbye to everyone, and it seemed many others were not ready to leave. Our family was exhausted, and we knew it was time to go. When we got home, family and close friends joined us. Bob and I were glad the house wasn't empty. Later that evening, we all ate leftovers from meals brought to us by friends and neighbors. We sipped vintage wine brought to us by our friends, Tony and Sharon, and we recounted the many memories and blessings of the day.

We also discussed our plans for the upcoming paddle out at Bolsa Chica State Beach. Everyone would meet before sunset at Lifeguard Station No. 17 where Kevin, his brothers, and buddies had surfed through the years. Eric told us our close family friend, Oz, had scheduled and paid for a helicopter and photographer to circle over the surfers and take pictures. David shared that a coworker would bring a large, white floral cross for Bob to fasten on Kevin's longboard he would ride. The day ended as it had begun with me asking God, "How can this be real? How can Kevin be gone? What good can possibly come from this exquisite pain? What are You doing?" Yes, I used the word exquisite because in the intense pain there was profound beauty and grace.

The next day, I tried to rest and enjoy being with family and friends, but grief cast a broad shadow over the day. I was restless and distracted by grief, and I would often have to say, "I'm sorry. What was that? What did you say?" Unable to be still for very long, I would aimlessly walk through the house, as though I was looking for something, and I would find myself in Kevin's room shutting the door to be alone and weep. Everyone was so loving and understanding of my need to be alone from time to time. Even if no one had understood, I would have had to be alone, giving myself permission to grieve. The day ended with Bob and me once again falling asleep in each other's arms as we cried.

On the day of the paddle out, I didn't feel well and dreaded going. I thought about staying home. But, then I told myself, *No! I have to do this for my son!* The event began at sunset, and I was surprised at the number of people waiting for us. The sight of the guys in their wetsuits and their surfboards lined upright in the sand triggered memories of the times I spent at the beach with the boys. The recollections also brought up an element of regret for how I had worked full-time and missed out on so many of those summer days at the beach with them. Regrets, I have very few, but that is definitely a significant one.

Soon Eric invited everyone to join him at the water's edge where he welcomed and thanked them for coming. He led us in a prayer asking God for His blessings as we gathered in that familiar and special place. Riding Kevin's longboard, Bob was the first in the water. One by one, our sons and the other surfers followed him. Once out into the calm, still ocean, they all sat up and formed a circle with Bob in the middle. The water and sand were cold under my feet as I attempted to make my way through the crashing waves to get closer to the circle. Venus was paddling through the waves as well but kept getting tossed around. She wasn't an experienced surfer, but she wanted so much to be out with the guys. Our lifelong friend, Jeff, tried to help her, but she wasn't able to make it to calmer waters, so he guided her back to shore. She and I looked at each other and shrugged our shoulders. At least we tried. We wanted to be a part of that circle very much.

Cold, shivering, and weary from the week, I thought about how surfers are a unique breed who possess courage, discipline, mental and physical agility, and a need for adventure. Surfing is their superpower. I've heard many quotes about surfing from Bob and our sons. "It isn't a sport; it's a way of life. To surf, you need three things: Your body, a surfboard, and a wave." Bob says it's the most challenging, relaxing, and exciting thing he's ever done.

Our young granddaughters, Nicole, Brianna, and Josslyn, brought a beach towel and stood beside me, jumping up and down in the water. Their youthful delight felt familiar and normal—it was good to feel something normal again. Looking out over the unreachable and endless horizon, I recalled our nephew, Eric

Carter, seeing the ocean for the first time when he was about three years old. He stood wide-eyed, and said to his mom, "That's *big* water. Where's the drain?" That memory made me giggle. It felt good to giggle.

As the sun began to set, each surfer left the circle to return to shore. It was like watching ships coming into a harbor. Bob, Eric, and David remained in the water for a while. It hurt to see only three when there had always been four. Only two sons when there had always been three.

At that moment, three seagulls flew over them as if to confirm that while Kevin would no longer be a part of their circle, he would forever be a part of them—and of me. Those three seagulls also reminded me of the Holy Trinity: Father, Son, and Holy Spirit. Again, as always, God's loving movements and actions were all around us.

Such movements and actions of God are often called "God winks." The term is defined as "an event or personal experience, often identified as coincidence, so astonishing that it is seen as a sign of Divine intervention, especially when perceived as the answer to a prayer" (Wiktionary). Blessings (God's protection and favor) and miracles (surprising and welcome events that are the work of the Divine) are evidence of God's intervention and happen every day in many ways: the physical aspects of nature, methods and systems of God's creation, the unconditional love of family and friends, the birth of a child, an illness healed, a broken marriage restored, or a tragedy that becomes a testament of praise.

Remembering what my dad told me as a girl—"It's good to know you have eyes to see and ears to hear"—I eagerly looked for and expected God's loving and Divine intervention throughout my journey of grief. He never disappointed me, and He keeps giving His love as he moves among us.

"Every good gift and every perfect gift is from above, coming down from the Father of lights, with whom there is no variation or shadow due to change." (Luke 6:8, ESV)

CHAPTER SEVEN

Dreams, Blessings, and Miracles

"God also testified to it by signs, wonders and various miracles, and by gifts of the Holy Spirit distributed according to his will." (Hebrews 2:4, NIV)

THERE'S A SONG WRITTEN BY MACK DAVID, Al Hoffman, and Jerry Livingston for the 1950 Disney movie, *Cinderella*, titled, "A Dream Is a Wish Your Heart Makes." When our sons were young, I would often say, "I'll see you in my dreams," after tucking them in bed.

As part of my heart's longing and calling out for Kevin, it is a blessing for me to dream a dream of him. Most of what I have dreamed is the same. Our family is in a place with friends, and I see him coming toward me from across the room. He smiles, gets close to me, hugs, holds me close, and tells me how glad he is to see me. In all of the dreams, he has a message for me, such as, "Mom, you look so tired. Get some rest. You are grieving too hard," or "You need to laugh a little. "Don't expect too much from other people. They can't do what God can do," or "I love you. I will always love you." These dreams have always come at just the right time, especially in moments of intense grieving and missing him. There are others who have had dreams about Kevin, and we all agree they are evidence of God's compassion and His assurance that Kevin is alive and well in His presence, and we are connected eternally.

Michele, who knew and loved Kevin all of his life, has told me she believes an angel of the LORD ministered to her at the paddle out. Overcome with grief, she walked away from the group, crying out to God, "Why would You take Kevin. Why now? He and Venus were going to be married in a few months. They are the sweetest couple. They belong together. Why are You doing this, God?"

Then, as she opened her eyes, she saw an older man standing next to her. "I have a message for you," he said.

Through tearful and suspicious eyes, she replied, "What? A message for me? From whom?"

"Yes," he said, "a message for you. I am here to tell you he is with God."

In the blink of an eye, Michele said the man was gone. In those few short seconds, she was comforted, and her faith and hope in God were strengthened. She also shared that she experienced an intense warming and a calming sense of peace. Kevin was with God. He was okay.

Kevin's fiancée, Venus, has shared a few dreams about Kevin. One was very troubling, as it revealed the depths of her pain, despair, and loneliness, but another was especially comforting. Here is what she told me, in her words, about that dream.

It has been some time since I have thought about this dream, perhaps by choice to protect my heart, as it is still so incredibly difficult to go back to this time. I thought it would somehow grow easier, but truth be told, it does not. The pain is still very much alive. I have just learned over the years to not let it be at the forefront of every thought.

However, when I do allow myself to remember, it is simultaneously always met with comfort and warmth encapsulated by peace, fondness, and a forever love that will always be remembered.

It is so easy to get caught up in the minutiae of each day that I rarely allow myself to sit in these memories and just be. Remembering and sharing this dream has allowed me to pause and bask in this space of reflection, feeling Kevin's love again. I remember this dream so vividly.

After Kev's passing, I wanted so desperately to have just a glimpse of him again. I have had a handful of dreams of him, however nothing as comforting and ethereal as this one.

It was sunset, and I was walking on a familiar, yet not quite defined, street. Out of nowhere, Kev appeared wearing light-tan, khaki pants; a white, buttoned, short-sleeve shirt; and his hair slightly longer—long enough to allow those natural waves and the sun to glisten through it. He did not appear to see or notice me, but I saw him and instantly had to catch up to him.

As fast as I walked along the sidewalk, for some reason I could not catch up to him. It was not as if he were walking faster or evading me, but I could not catch up to him.

As he approached a house, he turned right to enter it, and only then did we make eye contact. He simply smiled. He did not say a word, nor did I, but I knew I had to continue to follow him.

Inside the house were bare walls. There was no furniture, just a never-ending series of stairs. As he climbed the stairs, I followed and called out to him. Without a word, he turned around and smiled. He was so incredibly calm, focused, and, I could tell, determined to get where he was going.

The stairs seemed endless, and I remember feeling worried I would not be able to catch him or speak to him again. I had so many questions. I had to see his face. I had to not let him out of my sight.

I knew in my heart this would be the last time I would see him. I did not want him to slip away without being able to look at him, to hear his voice, to hold him. I could feel the anxiety rise within me that I might not get the chance. It was as if he could sense this in me, and suddenly he stopped at the top of the stair platform.

In front of him was a door. He opened it, and all I could see was pale, bright light everywhere that filled the stairway.

The light was all-consuming. I felt warm all over. It was in that moment I caught up to him. Sensing my worry and fear, he spoke to me, "It's going to be okay, Vee. I am fine. I am okay. I am happy. Everything is going to be okay. Everything is going to be okay." Then he held me and gave me the longest hug, and I felt instant warmth, reassurance, and peace. I did not, could not, would not let go of him. The hug lasted as long as it could, and then he said, "It's time to go. I have to go. Please do not worry about me. I am fine. I am going to be okay." He kept reassuring me over and over again.

The gentle and loving look in those green eyes was ever so comforting. I knew it was time. Slowly, I let go of him. As difficult as it was, I knew it was time. I did not want to let him leave my sight, but I knew he had a purpose. I could sense it. He was compelled to go. Watching him walk through that door, he seemed so happy, so content, so at peace. It was then I knew exactly where he was going and what he was trying to share with me. It was HEAVEN!

Bob dreamed he was paddling out like Kevin did at Dog Patch the day he died, except it was him on Kevin's longboard. As Bob struggled to paddle over, through, and under the pounding waves, he said his heart was beating very fast and he could hardly catch his breath.

Determined to make it through the surf, Bob wasn't strong enough in his dream to finish the ride. He said it helped him to better understand what had happened to Kevin.

I asked our sons, their wives, and our older grandchildren if any of them had dreamed of Kevin. Eric shared one that has stayed with him through the years.

I remember being in a funk about missing Kevin, and I dreamed I was sitting alone somewhere feeling very emotional. As I looked out into the distance, I could see a group of what I thought were kids playing. I couldn't see their faces, but I could tell by their body motions and demeanors everyone was having a great time and participating. I heard no words, only the sounds of laughter from far off in the distance.

Suddenly, one of the silhouettes of the group stopped playing and turned in my direction. I felt the individual could sense the feelings of despair I was experiencing about missing my brother. The silhouette began walking in my direction and entered into a light that exposed his face. It was Kevin.

He said no words, only smiled at me. Immediately, I felt

a sense of comfort and ease. He smiled at me for only a short moment, but it was enough time for me to see he was filled with extreme joy and happiness.

He turned away from me and began running back to the other silhouettes in the distance. Once he joined the group, I woke up from the dream, and I remember feeling extremely calm.

When Eric shared that dream with me, I remembered how, right after Kevin died, he told me, "Mom, I keep thinking of Kevin alone in a corner of Heaven saying, 'Where is my family? I miss my family.'" Surely Eric's dream was God's way of letting him know Kevin is not alone. He's happy and surrounded by "extreme joy and happiness."

David has had a few dreams of grieving and missing his brother. There was only one he thought was significant enough to share.

We were in a group of family and friends, and Kevin suddenly showed up. His skin was very tan, and his hair was longer than normal. Everyone rushed to him, and I asked him, "Where have you been? We thought you were dead." Kevin responded he had been on a surfing trip, and it was no big deal. "Dude, you've been gone a long time," I said.

Kevin was different; he was more relaxed than his normal self. He mingled with everyone like no time had passed at all. I watched him acting like there was no problem, and I got frustrated with him. "Dude, this is a big deal. We all thought you were dead!" Kevin just acted like there shouldn't be a problem and said, "Okay. Next time, I'll be sure to let everyone know where I'm going."

I remember feeling so relieved his passing didn't happen, and he was alive and with us.

Bob has had similar dreams where we are all together and everyone is talking about not knowing where Kevin is, wondering why he didn't tell anyone where he was going. Then, after being gone for a long time, he showed up all of a sudden. No one asked him where he had been. Everyone just seemed happy to see him again. But Bob was frustrated with Kevin, wondering why he didn't tell anyone where he had gone. Bob always woke up from those dreams sobbing into his pillow.

No one else in the family could recall a dream, but our oldest granddaughter, Nicole, told us about an interesting experience that happened about 17 years after Kevin died. She and her toddler son, Desmond, our great-grandson, were lying in bed together before he went to sleep. Lying on his back with his arms tucked behind his head, he looked up at the ceiling and said, "Are you all right up there, Kevin?" Nicole doesn't know what prompted him to say that. They hadn't been talking about his great-uncle Kevin.

His grandpa, Eric, sometimes takes Desmond to the cemetery when he places flowers at his brother's grave. He tells Desmond his uncle is in Heaven. Desmond once asked him, "If Kevin's in Heaven, why do we come here?" He was wise beyond his years, and it seems he has "eyes to see."

Throughout my life, I have seen much evidence of how God uses Divine interventions, dreams, blessings, and miracles to get our attention and to let us know He loves us, is omnipotent (with unlimited power), and omnipresent (present everywhere at any time). Mostly, I believe it is to let us know He sees and cares for us. The Bible is filled with accounts of signs, wonders, and miracles. The first miracle I experienced was on the day of my dad's funeral when I was 12 years old. Our family moved into our new house in Torrance, California, eight months before my dad died. One of the first things he did was plant a gardenia bush beside the front porch so we could enjoy its sweet aroma as the flowers bloomed. He chose a bush he thought looked healthy and paid more for it than he had budgeted. He followed the planting instructions and gardening guide to the letter and was excited about that gardenia blooming. It was one of my mom's favorite flowers, and her happiness was a priority for him.

Months went by, and there was not so much as a bud on the bush. One day, as I was sitting nearby on the porch while he watered it, Dad commented, "I hope this isn't a barren bush."

I asked him what he meant by that. "It might not have the seed of life in it. Or maybe I did something wrong in planting it." Another time I was standing next to him, as he bowed his head and prayed, "Lord of all living things. Breathe life into this dormant plant. You are the Creator and Sustainer of life." I silently asked God to answer his prayer.

Then, on the day of my dad's funeral, I walked out the front door and glanced over at the gardenia bush. To my absolute amazement and delight, there was a fully opened, gloriously white, perfectly formed, fragrant gardenia blooming. That flower wasn't there the day before when I sat on the porch next to the bush sobbing. I had checked that bush every day hoping for a bloom.

I was so excited the bush wasn't barren. It was alive and blooming. I knew my dad would have been thrilled—I realized God had heard and answered our prayers. That blooming gardenia was His gift, and His message to me was letting me know He hears and answers prayers in His time and according to His plan. I also believed He loved my dad, and He had breathed life into the gardenia bush in remembrance of him. It was also proof that He loved me, He loved my mom, and He loved Rusty. In that moment witnessing a miracle, I knew God was telling me my dad was fully alive, and life goes on.

Have you experienced the evidence of God's Divine intervention through dreams, blessings, and miracles? Do you look for and expect the loving movements and actions of God in your life? I hope and pray you do, because God is the One to bring out the miracle in us. We just need spiritual eyes to see, ears to hear, and hearts and souls that believe and trust in Him.

"I am the LORD, the God of all mankind. Is anything too hard for me?" (Jeremiah 32:27, NIV)

CHAPTER EIGHT

The Fires of
Unexpected Sorrow

"I have refined you, but not as silver; I have tried you in the furnace of affliction."　　　　　　　(Isaiah 48:10, ESV)

NO ONE WANTS TO SUFFER SORROW OR DIFFICULTY. But, it would be senseless to ask God to prevent these things, because difficulty, suffering, and sorrow are simply part of this life on earth. As Jesus accepted His fires of sorrow, He said, *"What shall I say? 'Father, save me from this hour?' But for this purpose I have come to this hour. 'Father, glorify your name'"* (John 12:27–28, ESV). When I think of Jesus, which I always do, especially when faced with suffering, sorrow, and difficulty, it seems to me if a person has not gone through the fires of sorrow, they might have little or no empathy for anyone who has. Spending my time in the fires of unexpected sorrow was the only way to truly find and understand God and my original self, as He formed me in my mother's womb.

Within weeks after Kevin's death, Bob and I were living parallel to each other, separated not by distance, but by how we were living with the loss of our son and grieving. We didn't talk to each other about what we were feeling and experiencing. Whenever I tried, Bob would say, "Men and women grieve differently." Not only did our son's death increase a sense of tension and disconnect, which had already started to creep into our relationship, but we also began to disagree and argue over simple and petty things. It seemed Bob needed to control everything, including me. There were many times when I was sure the loss of our son had dealt the final blow to our marriage. I even began to prayerfully consider a divorce.

The tension increased when Bob had to return to work after an unpaid bereavement leave where all of his vacation and sick days were depleted. He wasn't emotionally ready to go back to work as an air traffic controller, and I thought he might have resented me not working too, though I learned much later that was not the case. After one overheated argument, I was angry, frustrated, and overcome with grief. I ran into our bathroom, slammed the shower door, and the glass shattered in pieces all over the floor. Standing over the broken glass, I cried out to God, hoping Bob would hear me. "Do You see this? This is me! I'm broken into a thousand pieces."

We as individuals, our relationship, and our marriage were being threatened, and tested in the fires of unexpected sorrow. We were being scorched by the fire. Like teabags in hot water, the refining fire was revealing what was inside us. As the fire kept burning, it seemed as if I was failing in fulfilling my mom's hope and prayer that I would have a "holy grief." With no example of how to grieve in a healthy way, I wondered what grieving a holy grief really meant.

After my dad died, my mom grieved alone at night when my brother and I were asleep. We later learned she thought she was protecting us, trying to maintain some sense of normalcy. Not grieving together was confusing and troubling for Rusty and me. Mom didn't talk much about our dad or her grief, which caused me to wonder if she had really loved him at all. For years we were adrift in a sea of sorrow not sure who was steering our course.

Rusty and I were experiencing our own depths of sorrow, loneliness and fear. It would have been helpful if she had shared a measure of her grief. We could have comforted each other. Perhaps it wouldn't have taken as many years as it did for us to heal.

So, with no prior example of how to grieve a holy grief, I thought of Jesus and how He was a *"man of sorrows and acquainted with grief"* (Isaiah 53:3, ESV). Because He is holy, I decided He would be the One to teach me how to grieve in a holy way.

There were other mothers like me who were good examples. My precious, lifelong friend's son died by suicide at 19 years old. His death was followed by the death of another friend's 19-year-old son in a motorcycle accident. By entering into a measure of their grief and standing beside them at the edge of their sons' graves, I saw how they grieved.

My friend whose son died by suicide was devastated. Soon her grief became complicated and was intensified when she learned of her husband's past adulterous affairs. Because it was her nature to pick herself up and push through life's issues and circumstances, she tried to be strong. Yet, the harder she tried to be strong, the weaker and more troubled she became. Deeply hurt and injured, she admitted to making some unhealthy choices during that difficult time—but thankfully, she found her way back, and she came to describe herself as "a happy broken heart."

The other friend whose son died in the motorcycle accident was from a passionate, open, honest, and fun-loving Italian family. She had no trouble expressing her emotions or grief as she laid her body across her son's casket and sobbed.

When several people in the crowd stepped away from her, I moved closer. It seemed to me her response was appropriate not only for her but also for any mother experiencing the depths of sorrow caused by the loss of a child.

Perhaps the most compelling example of a mother's grief was following the suicide death of a coworker's only son. The family is from the Middle East, and I was invited to come to their house a few days after their son died. When I entered their home, a group of men were in one room, and the women were in another. A woman greeted me at the door and led me into the room where the women were gathered. She silently motioned for me to have a seat.

In the middle of the room was a large, colorfully upholstered ottoman. Sitting in the middle of the ottoman, shrouded under a black veil, was the grieving mother. Soon the woman who greeted me motioned for me to follow her to where the mother was sitting, telling me she had invited me to join her inside and under the veil of grief. She also instructed me to sit in silence. Slipping in under the veil was an unforgettable experience as the grieving mother pulled me close and wept. I cried with her. No words were spoken. None were necessary.

Being present and watching how these three precious women grieved proved very helpful to me when it was my turn at the grave and under the veil. Careful of who I invited in under my imaginary veil, there were very few who were willing to sit with me. Some ignored or refused my invitation. Being under the veil by myself was often lonely, but the LORD's presence comforted and strengthened me. He was *"acquainted with grief"* (Isaiah 53:3, ESV), and I allowed my tears to flow freely in His presence. They provided me an element of what I call "grief relief." God's Word confirms the value of our tears. *"You keep track of all my sorrows. You have collected all my tears in your bottle. You have recorded each one in your book"* (Psalm 56:8, NLT).

My daughter-in-law, Vel's, mom shared a poem she wrote about grief and how shedding "tears of deep grief" is part of God's design to allow the water of our heart and soul to become "clear and pure." I treasure her poem.

> The old faucet had been unused for decades
> But, she decided to turn the valve
> To give permission for the water to flow.
> Dark and rusty tears of deep grief and overwhelming
> sorrow streamed forth
> Until the water became clear and pure.
> —Lana Wicks-Gray © 2014

Though my tears are no longer "dark and rusty," and the water of my heart has become "clear and pure," I expect more tears, for surely there will be more trials, suffering, and grief ahead. When the refining fire is turned up on me, I often think of the recipe my dad shared with me when I was a young girl about how to cook a frog. Born and raised in the river bottom region of Mississippi, my dad caught, cooked, and ate his fair share of frogs. His recipe is a great metaphor for what can happen to someone who gets too comfortable in this world and possesses a cool, tepid, or lukewarm faith.

How to Cook a Frog

Place the frog in cool water.
Slowly, VERY slowly, turn up the heat.
Because the heating is gradual, the frog will get used to it.
Keep turning up the heat.
Boil the frog until dead and fully cooked.

"I know your deeds, that you are neither cold nor hot. I wish you were either one or the other!"

(Revelation 3:15, NIV)

"These trials will show that your faith is genuine. It is being tested as fire tests and purifies gold—though your faith is far more precious than mere gold."

(1 Peter 1:7, NIV)

CHAPTER NINE

Reflections of a Mother's Heart in Sorrow

"This is what the LORD . . . says: Write in a book all the words I have spoken to you."　(Jeremiah 30:2, NIV)

WRITING HAS ALWAYS BEEN AN IMPORTANT WAY for me to express my thoughts, feelings, and emotions. On my 10th birthday, my mom and dad gave me a pink leather diary, and for the next year that diary was my personal confidante.

Because it had a lock and key, I thought it was a safe place for me to share freely. When my little brother found the key, unlocked the diary, and read some of what I wrote, I felt violated and was angry at him, and we had a good talk about some of what he read and he said, "Sis, you write good. You should write a book."

Writing about my feelings and experiences was a way for me, as a young girl, to express myself in a way that allowed me to be completely honest with myself about what was going on inside that I never shared with anyone else.

As an adult, journaling became a normal part of my life. During the first few years of grieving the loss of my son, I journaled almost every day about what I was feeling, what I was experiencing. In preparing to write this chapter, I went through a box of journals and read through what I wrote, bringing yesterday's grief into the present.

Especially interesting to me were the Nov. 26 and Dec. 3, 2001, entries, which show how life can change in an instant. We never know what tomorrow will bring.

Nov. 26, 2001

Thank You, Lord, for the opportunity to work part-time with David. I look forward to this change of pace and something new to do. Help me to be a blessing to Dave and to the customers at the Cucina Deli.

Dec. 3, 2001

Father, I am celebrating life! There is a song in my heart, and I have joy. I praise You and am grateful that all is well with my soul!

Jan. 10, 2002

Our beautiful son died today. Death has come to our door and forced its way in. It is an unwelcome intruder. We have seen the face of death on the face of our child. Death comes to us all, but why Kevin and why now? Why before me, his mother? Why was he suddenly fit for Heaven? Did he learn the secret of life and fulfill his purpose on earth after only 28 years?

I want to scream. I cannot wrap my heart or my mind around the reality that my son is gone. I'm desperate to remember all the things that made him so sweet, sensitive, and special. It's hard to think. It's hard to find the words. How do I describe the effects of the wind? The spirit of such a beautiful soul.

He was adorable, precious, priceless, caring, loving, forgiving, cuddly, sweet, silly, gentle, kind, joyful, enthusiastic, passionate, loyal, true, playful, comforting, tender, fun, funny, wise, full of life and laughter. He is beautiful. He is mighty like a rose. Unforgettable.

Today changed everything, and I sit here now covered in ashes, wondering how I could ever experience God's great exchange as He gives *"beauty for ashes"* (Isaiah 61:3, NLT). Will I ever see and experience beauty again?

Exhausted and relieved that this day is over, I dread tomorrow. Oh, God, what have You done? Why have You taken my son? Did I take him for granted? Forgive me if

I took him for granted. Was I the mother he deserved? Why didn't I have a chance to tell him how much I love him this morning when he stopped by on his way to surf? Why didn't I get to say goodbye? Why do You keep taking people I love without me being able to say goodbye?

Jan. 15, 2002

Tonight, I stepped out into the courtyard and looked up at the night sky and cried, "Where are you, my child?" In despair, I then cried out to God, "Won't You change your mind and give him back to us?" Moonbeams shone down on me and the North Star seemed to point the way to Heaven. How far and in what dimension is Heaven? Where is my child dwelling? What is he doing? God, I cry out to You in pain and sorrow. Do You see me? Do You hear me?

Calling Out

Where are you, my child?
Are you near to me somehow?
Do you know how much I miss you?
How empty the house is now?

What I know about Eternal Life assures me
You are in better hands than mine
Now, you are strong and mighty
Full of radiant light.

In that place where it's always day
No need for sleeping or for night.

I am weeping.
You are laughing.
I am crippled with grief.
You are running on streets of gold
I am numb.
You are fully alive.
I am in despair.
You are in perfect peace.

My heart is broken in pieces.
My soul is weary and worn.
Will I survive this grief
Without losing hope or wishing I'd never been born.

You are in your eternal home now.
When will I join you?
Will it be soon or quite a while?

Determined to hold onto my faith
Believing without a doubt
One day we will stand together forever
Understanding what suffering and pain was all about.

—Angie Ford-Green © 2002

Precious Son,

Who greeted you at Heaven's gate? Whom did you see and meet first? Was it the angel Gabriel, Michael the Archangel, Jesus? Have you met some of our family? Were my dad and your other grandparents and great-grandparents there to greet you? What about Mary, Jesus' mother? Have you spent time with Abraham, Isaac, and Jacob? Moses, Elijah, and the Apostles?

What's it like to be in the company of a multitude of saints, angels, and Heavenly creatures? I want eyes to see what you are seeing!

Feb. 2, 2002

I turned off the porch light tonight for the first time in years. It was painful. It didn't feel right to turn off the light that welcomed and guided you and your brothers' steps home in the dark.

I'm in such a dark place tonight. As quickly as I turned off the light, I turned it back on again.

I'm not ready to accept that I will never hear your footsteps coming up the walkway, see you walk in the front door, or hear you say, "Mom, I'm home."

All of the words penned in my journals record but a small portion of what I was feeling and experiencing.

Some days my spirit was lifted and I was stronger. Other days I would be cast down and in despair.

I have known no greater joy than being a mother, and the labor pains of childbirth cannot compare with the pain of suffering the loss of my child. Will this pain ever end?

May 12, 2002

Today is Mother's Day, and I heard from everyone but Kevin.

I went to a retreat for grieving moms last weekend, and it helped to prepare me for today. I was blessed today by my husband, sons, and grandchildren's sweet and thoughtful cards, hugs, and gifts, but there was a shadow of grief hanging over us all.

Thankful for my sons, Eric and David, their wives and children, but there is a hole in my heart now with Kevin's name on it. A hole that might never close completely. My greatest fear now is that there will be other holes in my heart with other names of those I love, "Oh, God, please. Don't take any of my children before me.

And, yet, I thank you, Father, for fulfilling my young girl's dream to be a wife and a mother. You have blessed me, and our family quiver is full, but it hurts so badly that we are less a beloved arrow now gone.

June 30, 2002

People going about their normal lives hurt and offend me, and that troubles me. Not normally a selfish or self-absorbed person, is it wrong for me to feel this way? Is this going to be part of my new normal? Will I be jealous and envious of other families that don't have to live with this loss of a child?

Dec. 8, 2002

Why haven't I written in my journal since June? I have no recollection of what I have been doing these past six months other than grieving.

Today, would be Kevin's 29th birthday. How are we to remember and celebrate this day that was once marked with joy and celebration?

It hurts so much that there will be no more birthday celebrations with him. Should I bake a cake? Why can't I remember his favorite flavor? What am I thinking? There is no way to celebrate as we have in the past. We can't have a party without the guest of honor. No one wants to try to celebrate without our party guy.

Though he wasn't happy that his sister-in-law Vel's birthday is the same day as his, I'm thankful we have her to celebrate, and I believe it is part of God's plan for us to have her in our family, born on the same day as Kevin.

My heart is full of gratitude and grief today. It is a strange duality becoming more and more familiar to me. "Father, please call my son out of the crowd of Heaven and tell him I love him, and I am remembering the day he was born when I told Bob to *look at our beautiful son, he's Kevin from Heaven.* God, do You celebrate earthly birthdays in Heaven somehow?

Dec. 30, 2002

It is the end of 2002, and I'm glad this year is over and gone. Daisy Catchings-Shader, cofounder of Umbrella Ministries, has told me to expect the second year of grieving to be worse than the first. How can that be? A year worse than this one? Maybe it was just true for her.

As I say, "Goodbye, 2002," I will remember it as a horrible year, a year that changed everything—and not for the better.

What will 2003 be like for me, for Bob, for our family? Once again I'm at a place in my life with so many questions. Will it be a year worse than this one? What memories will we make? What trials and challenges will we face? Will we stand strong? Will we fall apart? Will we continue to grieve day after day, week after week, month after month? Will this pain and sorrow ever subside? Will I survive? Will my marriage survive? What will happen next?

These and so many other worrisome questions have replaced my positive attitude looking ahead. Never before have I been so skeptical, untrusting, and disappointed in people. Before now, I was filled with love, hope, and joy, anticipating what might be around the corner, believing God is always before me, behind me, and beside me. What is happening to me? Am I losing hope? Am I losing myself? Am I already lost?

CHAPTER TEN

Say What?

"Pleasant words are a honeycomb, sweet to the soul and healing to the bones." (Proverbs 16:24, KJV)

IF EVERYONE WHO HAS EXPERIENCED LOSS GOT TOGETHER to share what people have said to them after the loss of someone they love, lively, even laughable, conversations would follow. Well-meaning people can say silly and some-times stupid things to those who are suffering and grieving.

For example, a woman I didn't know told me at my dad's funeral, "Now, Angie, you know your daddy is in Heaven. Keep the faith. Be a good girl and help your mother."

What? Why was she concerned about me not keeping the faith? Was I going to no longer be a good girl? How was I supposed to help my mother? I was 12 years old.

Those woman's words were not comforting. They were confusing, troubling and made me angry. In that moment, the line spoken in the Disney movie, *Bambi*, by the little rabbit Thumper's mom came to my mind, and I almost told her, "If you can't say something nice, don't say nothing at all!" I guarded my tongue. Dad would have been proud of me.

When I was 18, I visited my cousin, Diana, in the hospital after she suffered the stillborn death of her firstborn daughter. Young and detached from her grief, I chattered like a chipmunk about anything and everything. At one point, she looked at me with gentle, tearful eyes that said she knew I was trying to distract her, but it wasn't helping. I was so ashamed, I cut the visit short and all but ran out of the hospital like something was chasing me. My pathetic attempt to somehow take her mind off of her grief was naïve and wrong, and it taught me a very important lesson.

Words don't matter to someone who is grieving. Being present and expressing a simple "I'm sorry" is enough.

Though most people are genuinely sympathetic, they might lack empathy: the ability to actually feel and enter into another person's pain and sorrow. In times of grieving, we need to be more careful to truly make sure our heart (not just our brain) is engaged before putting our mouth in gear.

With so many attempts by people to give me advice and encouragement that fell flat, I began to make a list of some of the well-intended things people said to me following Kevin's death. I share this list not to judge or criticize anyone. It provides examples of what *not* to say to someone who is experiencing grief. It is a long list. Some of it might surprise you, as it surprised me.

"It was his time."

"Time heals all wounds."

"At least you have other children and grandchildren."

"I'll call you and stay in touch." (They did neither.)

"You are the strongest person I know. I couldn't handle this."

"I'm afraid this is going to happen to me."

"You know he is with God!"

"Why are you depressed? Don't you believe he is in Heaven?"

"He was a Christian, wasn't he?"

"You need to get up, get dressed, and get moving."

"The Bible says we should cry when a child is born and rejoice when he dies."

"You've got to get over this."

"God never gives us more than we can bear."

"Maybe you should get a puppy."

"You have lost your joy."

"You look like you are eighty years old."

"You look like a drowned kitten."

"Everything happens for a reason."

"God needs him more than we do."

"He's in a better place."

"I am going to hang up now. Call me back when you stop crying."

"I'm grieving too. Our dog died last week."

"If I went through everything you are going through, I'd probably kill myself."

"Others may have it worse than you do."

"At least your son didn't kill himself or die from a drug overdose."

"You've got to snap out of it. It's been a year!"

"Stop crying. If you believe he's in Heaven, why are you crying?"

"You are a hot mess."

"I don't know how to help you. Tell me what to do."

"How long do you think you will grieve like this?"

"Do you think Kevin would want you to go on like this?"

"Aren't you getting tired of being sad?"

"I don't think it's a good idea for us to talk about him."

"Try to forget about this. Have another glass of wine."

"You believe all things work together for good, right?"

"This too will pass. Life goes on."

"You will get through this—you are a beast!"

The last statement, "you are a beast," made me feel like some kind of she-creature. Yes, I am a strong woman, and I did survive and made it through the most difficult times of grieving, but I am certainly not a beast. Just like what I said to my cousin in the hospital, words meant to help were actually hurtful.

While much of what people shared with me was kind, compassionate, and encouraging, even then they spoke in platitudes, defined in *Webster's Dictionary* as "remarks or statements that have been used too often to be interesting or thoughtful." In my most desperate moments of sorrow and pain, platitudes only added insult to injury.

The comments made by well-meaning Christians wounded and hurt me the most. Their Bible passages fell flat. God's Word was hidden in my heart. What I needed most from my brothers and sisters of faith was for them to connect, engage, and talk with me as a fellow human being, not as a preacher or teacher. It was offensive when they questioned or challenged my hope and trust in God, and their exhortations to remain faithful to God seemed callous and insensitive. Anyone who knew anything about me at all was well aware of my faith in the LORD and how I knew He was with me. The difference between Him and those who preached to me was how He comforted and accepted me just as I was.

Being slow to speak (James 1:19–20) and speaking words of compassion, comfort, hope, and understanding

(1 Thessalonians 5:11) to someone grieving is vitally important. There's an old saying, "Sticks and stones may break my bones, but words can never hurt me," but that is simply not true. Words can and do hurt, possibly more than broken bones.

It is common for those of us who are grieving to pull away, withdraw, and even isolate ourselves when we need people most. Being sensitive and empathetic, giving people permission to grieve, and remaining close and trying to understand what we are going through is what is most needed and welcomed.

In the end, God's voice was and has always been the most comforting, loving, and reliable voice I need to hear. He always knows what to say and when to say it. I want to be more like Him.

"If I speak in the tongues of men or of angels, but do not have love, I am only a resounding gong or a clanging cymbal."
(1 Corinthians 13:1, NKJV)

CHAPTER ELEVEN

A Call of Love

"My love for you is at all times as a flame of fire. My ardor never cools. My longing for your love and affection is deep and constant . . . You will experience resurrection life and peace; the joy of the Lord will become your strength; and wells of salvation will be opened within you."

—Frances J. Roberts, "The Call of Love,"
Come Away My Beloved

AFTER KEVIN'S DEATH, THE INITIAL OUTPOURING of concern quickly subsided, leaving Bob and me alone to grieve.

Everything was different. Everything had changed.

Nothing was the same. Nothing would ever be the same.

There were many days when the grief overwhelmed, crippled, and paralyzed me. Getting up and aimlessly wandering around the house, I often did not get dressed, fix my hair, put on makeup, or do basic household tasks and routines. It seemed my only routine was to lose track of time and weep uncontrollably.

One day when Bob came home from work, he asked, "Why are you still in your pajamas? Why haven't you combed your hair? Have you eaten anything? What have you been doing all day?"

"I don't know," I said through fresh tears. His body language told me he was not only concerned for me but also frustrated with me. The day had passed quickly, and I had been immersed and wallowing in grief, unaware of my appearance, of my need for food or water—of anything but my grieving.

I looked at myself in the wall mirror. It was a shock. Not only was I unkempt and disheveled but also my face was drained of color. The dark circles under my eyes made me look like a battered, worn-out old woman. What a pitiful sight I was sitting on the floor in front of the mirror with my head hanging down in embarrassment and shame.

"Mirror, mirror, on the wall," I mumbled. "Who's the saddest, ugliest woman of all? It's me!"

All I could do was weep. How grotesque and weak I

must have seemed to Bob. He was getting up and going to work every day, and I couldn't seem to do any part of my normal routine. In that, my lowest point, it seemed God lifted my head, told me He loved me, and that I was beautiful to *Him*. Out of the ugliness of grief, His love called out, *"Come to me, all who labor and are heavy laden, and I will give you rest"* (Matthew 11:28, ESV). Once again His Word spoke to me, declaring that His love and rest were what I needed most. Though I did not feel beautiful, I believed God saw me through His eyes of love. In receiving and accepting His never-failing, never-ending love, there was no longer room for shame or embarrassment.

God's call of love reminded me who I am—a Child of God and a Daughter of the King whose identity is in Christ Jesus. Taking a deep breath, I rose from the floor in front of the mirror stronger, unashamed, and with hope. I took a shower, got dressed, combed my hair, put on some makeup, and walked into the kitchen to prepare a meal.

From that day forward, I was warmed and over-whelmed by God's love! The color returned to my face, and the dark circles under my eyes disappeared. To experience His touch changed everything. It had always been His love I longed for and needed most.

Going deeper into a more intimate relationship and dependence on Him was the beginning of deep healing within me. Hope floated to the top of the pool of sorrow I had been swimming in up to that point. God called me out of the shadows of death, the ugliness of grief, into His glorious light.

He was all I needed. He was all I would ever need. The windows of my soul were wide open to Him.

"Within our heart is a longing—a profound cry of the soul for something our theologies can only point us to, never replace. Intimacy with God. Something that has no human or earthly substitute . . . God speaks to us through human and earthly means. He stands at the windows of the easily overlooked and the unlikely, tapping at the pane. He beckons us to places of encounter where we learn how well he understands the language of our hearts. At unexpected windows of the soul, we hear the voice of God."

—Ken Gire, *Windows of the Soul*

"Rise up, my love, my fair one, and come away."
(Song of Solomon 2:10, KJV)

"The LORD's unfailing love surrounds the one who trusts in him."   (Psalm 32:10, NIV)

"Follow the way of love."   (1 Corinthians 14:1, NIV)

CHAPTER TWELVE

Be Still and Know

"I will lead her into solitude and there I will speak to her heart."
(Hosea 2:14, NIV)

NOT ONLY DID THE LORD CALL ME BY HIS LOVE but He also led me into silence and solitude. I was certain He purposefully placed me in this unfamiliar space, similar to how He placed Jonah in the belly of a big fish when Jonah tried to run away in disobedience. I had no inclination or desire to run away from God, but from grief. Every emotion, thought, and action was to find a way to escape from the pain and sorrow. Grief and the clamoring sounds of the world cluttered my mind and disturbed my soul.

In my grieving, I spent a great deal of time alone in silence and stillness. To my surprise, that space became my personal prayer closet where my mind and will were calmed, soothed, and refreshed.

Too often in the past, I was like a bumping car in an arcade. It seemed I was always bumping into people and circumstances, or they were bumping into me. In silence, stillness, and solitude, I experienced the calming spirit of God, peace, and rest. If Kevin had not died, I wonder if I would have kept bumping into life rather than resting and refreshing in God's love and peace.

How about you? Are you bumping into people, issues, and circumstances? Do you need to spend some time in your big, fish-shaped, prayer closet?

A friend of a friend wrote a book, *The Silver Pen: Sound and Silence,* where the author shares the joy she has experienced in silence and solitude. Her grandparents were deaf. In a close relationship with them is where she says she received the *gift of silence.* I too had a close relationship with my grandparents who lived a very quiet and simple life. Until I was 15 years old, I spent many Friday nights and Saturdays with them where I could rest and refresh. Perhaps, though a lively extrovert, I intuitively wanted a quieter, simpler life too.

An introvert naturally seeks silence and solitude. Extroverts are typically more energized and happiest when we are interacting with people and the world around us. The idea of sitting in silence, or being alone, is not necessarily appreciated by extroverts, making us antsy and feeling we have to be doing something every waking moment of the day. As a young girl growing up in a very active and busy family, I enjoyed times when I could be alone to think, imagine, and dream. These times were few and far between. It wasn't until Kevin died that I realized I needed to be still and alone to slow down and reduce the anxiety caused by grief. Sitting in silence helped to calm my emotions and settle my mind, and believe me when I say *my mind needed to settle down.*

In the silence of my solitude I found that Albert Einstein was right when he said, "The monotony and solitude of a quiet life stimulates the creative mind." There are many wise comments and quotes about silence and solitude, including the following.

"Without great solitude, no serious work is possible."
—Pablo Picasso

"Nothing strengthens authority so much as silence."
—Leonardo da Vinci

"Be still and know that I am God."   —Psalm 46:10, NIV

Grief forced me to be still, withdraw and quiet the voices and noise of the world so I could embrace the *gift of silence.* Learning to enjoy silence and being alone has given me the opportunity to connect to my inner self and to the invisible reality of the presence of God who whispers to me.

What happens to you when you are alone and in silence? Do you fidget? Are you antsy to get up and do something or to go someplace? Are you able to be still and just breathe? Are you afraid of silence? Are you afraid to be alone? If you are afraid of silence and solitude, why do you think that is true for you?

These are challenging questions my bereavement counselor asked me in the first session we had together after Kevin died. My answers surprised me. *I do not like to be still. I avoid being alone. I don't like my own company.*

Being alone with grief forced me to consider why I wasn't comfortable with silence and solitude. The truth is I was disappointed and bored with myself. Living a life that didn't seem to fit who I really was, I came to understand I had been trained to be an extrovert by my mom, but God had created me to be more reflective and contemplative. After that personal revelation, I began to seek silence and solitude, and I became very comfortable alone with myself.

A quiet stillness permanently resides within me. Now, I long for moments when I can be alone with the presence of God filling the silent stillness.

"*Silence slides in and stillness quenches my thirst for peace as I am lulled by the softness of His rain drip dance, His lullaby slows. Sweet peace has thoroughly anointed my soul, and placed words of peace into my heart.*"

—Jan Voth Dubbs, "The LORD's Lullaby," *The Silver Pen*

"*Arise my darling, my beautiful one, and come along. For behold, the winter is past.*"

(Song of Solomon 2:10–11, BSB)

CHAPTER THIRTEEN

A Glimpse of Heaven

"For I consider that the sufferings of this present time are not worth comparing with the glory that is to be revealed to us."
(Romans 8:18, ESV)

JUST THREE MONTHS AFTER KEVIN DIED, I WAS hospitalized for what doctors thought was a heart condition, instead I was diagnosed with shingles due to stress. My primary doctor encouraged me to get away to rest, and I thought of St Mary's Retreat House in Santa Barbara. For a few years, it had been a tradition for me to travel there around my birthday in October. I decided to make the trip in May shortly after Mother's Day.

From Friday after dinner to lunch on Sunday, guests at St. Mary's are supposed to be silent. My nature was to talk, so having to be silent for two days was challenging, but it was good for my soul. If we had to talk, we could go up to the "Big House," where Anglican nuns made themselves available for visits and spiritual direction.

The nuns also led worship services at morning, noon, and eventide, as they referred to the evening services. Being intentional about attending all three services each day introduced me to the Anglican form of worship that included liturgy, homilies, candles, incense, litany, and a cappella songs of praise. That style and form of worship was new to me and stimulated and satisfied my senses and enhanced my adoration of Christ.

The nuns were dear and thoughtful, and I admired their devotion and commitment to Christ, one another, and their guests. The nun I remember best was Sister Angela. She reminded me of my grandmother. We connected right away.

Sister Angela had been married for many years and had middle-age sons. After her husband died, she decided to devote the rest of her life to serving God and others within a covenant community. She had suffered much loss throughout her life, and she openly shared how she believed God used her pain and suffering to make her more aware of the sufferings of Jesus and others. Before entering the covenant community, she told me, "I was very self-absorbed and really knew nothing about the sufferings of Christ and others."

During one of our visits, I told her I was having trouble being quiet. Her response was simple, "Dear one. Stop talking." That is Sister Angela, a no-nonsense woman with candor, common sense, wisdom, and a sense of humor surpassed only by her great faith and devotion to God. The times we spent together at St. Mary's were a significant part of my healing from my wounds of grief. And, she was a role model for me of how pain and sorrow can be used to help others.

Sister Angela has since gone on to be with God. She is one of the people I will look for when I get to where she is now. I saw Jesus in her warmth, the twinkle in her eyes, her beautiful smile, and a servant's heart acquainted with grief. I will never forget her.

On the last day at St. Mary's, I recall sitting alone on the patio at sunset. The sight of houses on the hills across from where I sat caught my attention and transported me to another time. Another place. Out of nowhere came an image of Kevin looking out a window from the hills of Heaven, and I recalled Jesus telling His disciples, *"In My Father's house are many mansions, if it were not so I would have told you. I go to prepare a place for you"* (John 14:2, NKJV). Though comforting to think of Kevin in Heaven, it was disturbing to consider the chasm and distance between us, and I recalled what a pastor once said. "Heaven is just in another room, another dimension. It's closer than we know." His words were comforting. I hoped they were true.

The sunset that night was a show of brilliant shades of soft white, orange, blue, and pink. Spring was in the air. Flowers were in full bloom. Birds were singing their nighttime songs to their Creator. For months after Kevin died, I had not noticed or appreciated the colors of a sunset, blooming flowers, and birdsongs.

The weekend at St. Mary's was made to order. The time spent in silence and daily worship refreshed my weary soul. The houses on the hill at sunset provided a glimpse of Heaven that opened the eyes of my heart wide and clear. As I started to board the train that would take me back home, I paused before moving forward. I wasn't ready to go back to the new normal and grief-stricken routine. I wanted to turn and go back to St. Mary's, and I almost did. In that moment, I could hear Sister Angela say, "It's time, dear one. Your husband and your family need you. Go home where you belong. Be light and salt. Don't hold on to pain and suffering. Lay it down. Let it go." *"Live by faith, not by sight"* (2 Corinthians 5:7, NIV).

CHAPTER FOURTEEN

A Three-Stranded Cord

"A person standing alone can be attacked and defeated, but two can stand back-to-back and conquer. Three are even better, for a triple-braided cord is not easily broken."
(Ecclesiastes 4:12, NLT)

OUR THREE SONS HAD ALWAYS BEEN VERY CLOSE with a bond that is strong and true. As tender warriors and beautiful souls, their personalities and sense of adventure and play created quite a story of brotherly love and fun in action.

Each with unique personalities, they had always been like The Three Musketeers: "All for one and one for all!" Eric, the oldest, was the ringleader of their band of brothers. It was his nature, and I think he believed it was his responsibility, to protect his brothers, keep them entertained with some mischief, and challenge their courage and manhood whenever he thought it was necessary. Eric also enjoyed teasing and taunting them with tricks, like turning off the main water while they were showering or telling David, suited up with a football helmet and ball in hand, to "close your eyes and charge" before stepping aside to let his brother slam into the stone wall. (I was *very* angry at him for doing that.) Nevertheless, knowing how much he loved them, David and Kevin would have followed Eric anytime and anywhere without hesitation. They were not only brothers but they were also best friends!

Loyal to one another, honest, supportive, and encouraging, nothing would sever the bond they shared because they all agreed they were and are part of one another.

A week or so after the memorial service, one of Kevin's close friends, Dave, called and told me he would like to stop by for a visit. He had something he wanted to share about a conversation he'd had with Kevin. Of course, I told him to come over. I longed to hear stories about Kevin.

He and Kevin had been working out with weights in the garage when Dave asked him, "So, Kevin, be honest. You and your brothers aren't really as close as you seem, right? Most of the brothers I know are very competitive and even jealous of one another. They fight for attention, wanting to be the favorite son, the alpha dog. Isn't that really how it is between you and your brothers? Come on. You can tell me the truth."

Dave smiled as he continued. "Kevin replied, 'That's not us!' When I asked why, he said, 'My brothers and I are like one person. Eric is the serious one. David is the sensitive one. I'm the silly one. When you put us together, we make a whole person.'"

I loved hearing that! There is nothing that blesses me more as their mother than to know my sons deeply loved and would take a bullet for one another. Since they were very young, I always thought of them like a three-stranded cord. Together, they could face anything, stand for or against anything, do anything, and accomplish anything. Together, they were strong.

When they were little, I described their personalities as being like Winnie the Pooh characters. Eric was like Christopher Robin and sometimes Eeyore. David was like Tigger, full of energy and always wanting to have fun. Kevin was like Pooh, not with a pooch belly, but soft and cuddly. Their bond as brothers and friends was evident to anyone who knew them, and they had a reputation for being The Green Boys; if you messed with one, you would have to mess with the others.

Watching the three of them growing up was my life's greatest blessing. What a joy it was to know how much they loved one another and how they went together like bread, peanut butter, and jelly, their favorite sandwich. I couldn't imagine one without the others—and never would I have imagined one of them would die. Rather, I saw them dying side by side in a war, standing together against all odds. Really, I envisioned a lifetime of them working, playing, worshipping, raising their families, growing old, and burying Bob and me. They belonged together. They fit. They were a three-stranded cord.

So, after Kevin died, Eric and David suffered deeply. Their little brother delighted them and made our family complete. His loss took a big piece of his brothers' hearts with him—and they would never be the same. Sometime after Kevin's death, our family gathered at our house for a meal. It was awkward and painful. We were very much aware of the empty chair at the table.

At one point, David got up and walked out the front door. I waited a few minutes before I went looking for him, and I found him sitting on the curb in front of the house looking out at the cul-de-sac where he, his brothers, and the neighborhood kids had played for years. I sat down next to him.

"Are you okay, son?" I asked. "Are you remembering you and your brothers playing in the cul-de-sac?"

"Yes, Mom," he said. "I don't understand why this happened. I've lost a piece of myself."

How I desperately wanted to take away his pain. I nudged closer and took his hand in mine. "Son, some of my favorite memories are of the summer months when you and your brothers would stay outside until the streetlights came on playing and laughing. Remember how your dad or I would call each one of you by name, telling you it was time to come inside?"

Head down, David nodded. I carried on.

"Remember also how it was always you who would plead for five more minutes, and we would give you five more minutes until it was time to come home?" Again, he nodded. "This is how I think of Kevin's death. God determined there were no more minutes for him on this earth. It was time for him to come home—to his eternal home."

As I leaned into my grieving son, I looked up at the stars and imagined Kevin in Heaven, remembering his brothers and the bond of love they shared. I quietly prayed, "Oh, LORD, please call Kevin out of the crowd of Heaven and tell him we all love him so much. Bless and heal Eric and David who have been left behind."

As David and I wept together, much of our grief was because their three-stranded cord was physically severed, and my belief that their bond was eternal, and would never end, comforted my mother's heart.

"So, we fix our eyes not on what is seen, but on what is unseen, since what is seen is temporary, but what is unseen is eternal." (2 Corinthians 4:18, NIV)

CHAPTER FIFTEEN

Puppies and Puddles

"I am afflicted and needy; May the Lord be mindful of me. You are my help and my savior; Do not delay, my God."

(Psalm 40:17, NASB)

LIKE UNTRAINED PUPPIES, BOB AND I MADE a mess of the first few years of grieving. The first year was hard and is still a blur. Our entire family was in shock and traumatized. I kept telling myself things would get better with time. I really didn't think they could get any worse, but I was wrong. The second year was much worse than the first, just as Daisy Catchings-Shader had said.

Immersing myself in God's Word, I also searched for grief-related resources. I needed someone to guide me through my grief and to talk about what was happening to me. Mostly, I needed to talk to Bob and mourn with him, but he showed no outward sign of grieving. He shut down and seemed indifferent, uncaring, and unloving toward me. We were not a comfort to each other, and tension continued to build between us. Whenever I asked him to share some-thing of what he was feeling and experiencing, he'd reply, "I'm okay. I'm a man, and you're a woman. We're different. It doesn't help me to talk about it."

Years later, I asked him why he didn't grieve with me. "I had to be strong because of my job," he said. "People's lives were at stake, and I had to financially provide for us. Everything felt out of my control, and I tried to at least control things at work and home." As an air traffic controller at Long Beach Airport, Bob was at one of the five busiest airports in the country. The year Kevin died, there were more than 400,000 flights in and out of that airport. Bob set aside his grief and ignored mine, not realizing how much I needed him. If we had been at the place we are now in our relationship, things would have been very different and much better for us.

Back then, we were in real trouble as a couple. I had heard 80 percent of parents who suffer the loss of a child get divorced, and I was sure we were going to fall into that category. I had little hope we were going to make it. Especially troubling was watching Bob shut down emo-tionally and use alcohol more than before. His DNA is 80 percent Irish, so he's always enjoyed beer and a stiff drink now and then, but he sometimes drank too much. Under the influence of alcohol, Bob was a very different person, often unreasonable, and mean to me in private. After a night of heavy drinking, he generally had no remembrance of, or remorse for, how he had acted. It felt like I was living with two different people, and I didn't like or trust the one under the influence. He never thought it was a "big deal," but it was for me.

When he claimed men and women were different and grieved differently, I wondered if it was true. Were other husbands like mine? Maybe he was right. I began to think all men were able to compartmentalize and detach emotionally.

So, while Bob struggled to cope with the loss of our son, I was an emotional wreck, unstable, and hyper-sensitive. Everything and everyone seemed different. I was also experiencing an intense menopause. Nothing felt normal. There were times I thought I was losing it. People close to me thought so too. I never thought specifically about suicide, but there were times I asked God, "Please take me out of here! You took my dad and my son. Take me too!" At times, the changes in my life were confounding. Pain, sorrow, and confusion consumed me.

I was relieved to find a study by The Compassionate Friends from 2006, showing parental divorce following the death of a child was actually only about 16 percent. It also stated that less than half of those who were divorced following the death of their child felt the death had contributed to the disintegration of the marriage. Through bereavement counseling and spiritual direction from others, many of the painful knots forged inside me began to untangle. I also began to withdraw and protect myself from toxic relationships and anyone who didn't seem to really care about me.

Needing to connect to the people who were closest to me, I decided to pretend everything was fine, and things calmed down for a while. Determined to put on a happy face and set aside my grief, I told myself, "Happy wife, happy life," or "If Mama's happy, everybody's happy." "Don't have expectations, and you won't be disappointed." "Smile though your heart is breaking." Pretending everything was fine didn't work or change a thing—and neither did starting to drink socially to fit in. In fact, pretending and drinking made things much worse. Trying to be strong, faking my way through grief, and going along to get along were huge mistakes.

When Bob and I reflect on those troubled times, we very much wish we could have a do-over. We realize we were in survival mode, reacting rather than responding, and functioning with an appease, withdraw, or fight-or-flight mentality. We didn't know there was a better way to grieve. We didn't know a healthy path to healing should begin with compassion, honesty, patience, and understanding while respecting and honoring our unique differences as individuals.

In our grieving, affection and peace seemed elusive, and we both said and did a lot of things that were very hurtful. Once, I told Bob I had never been happy married to him.

"I don't believe you!" he said. "I've seen you happy. If that's really true, then you have done a good job of acting and pretending."

My hateful response was, "Well, you know me. I was groomed and trained to be an actor performing on stage, so believe me when I tell you I've never been happy with you. Never!"

Shaking his head in disbelief, he looked as though I had delivered a deadly stab in his heart. At that point, I didn't care. I wanted to hurt him. He was hurting me, and I had remembered a dream from several years before.

We were on a battlefield dressed in 16th-century armor surrounded by a multitude of enemy armies. The armor and sword in my hand were heavy. Enemy warriors were pressing in on us. We were fighting for our lives, and I was sure we would die. As I struggled to stay upright, with tears streaming down my face and blurring my vision, Bob turned toward me and stabbed me in my right side. Shocked, sobbing, and in pain, I dropped my sword and yelled at him, "You're going to kill me!"

As I reached down to cover my wound, I turned to look behind me, and I saw the commander of our army standing on top of a hill overlooking the battlefield. He was tall, fully armored, and a bright light was shining down on him. Running as fast as I could, I reached the top of the hill and fell down at the commander's feet. Wrapping my arms around his legs, I cried, "Please don't send me out there again! I'm going to die! My husband is going to kill me."

Placing his hand gently on my shoulder, my commander replied, "I never sent you to fight on the battlefield. You went out on your own. Stay here with me."

Had Bob and I had stayed as close to each other as we were right after Kevin died, we believe our battles would have been minimal. If we had admitted our need for help and guidance through our pain and sorrow, we might not have fought against each other at all.

It seems to me Bob and I were like out-of-control, untrained puppies, nipping at each other, constantly fighting, and leaving messes and puddles of wasted time and opportunities everywhere. Not understanding we were grieving differently, we were ill-equipped to know how to grieve together. Fortunately, we experienced a turning point when we came to terms with our individual grieving needs and honored our differences. Thankfully, when I think of puddles now, I recall a special rainy day when our young family played in the rain at a park, All of us sliding down slides and landing and jumping in puddles. That is a very good memory.

Our marriage has been tested, refined, and resurrected. Now, whenever things get messy, we look to our commander, Jesus Christ, inviting Him to help us. It's obvious to both of us that God didn't want us divorced. He never gave me permission to get a divorce, despite the many times I begged Him to release me, and I questioned why He wanted me to stay in a marriage filled with tension, misunderstandings, and heartache.

Through the years since Kevin died, Bob and I have reaffirmed our love and promise "till death do we part." It would have crushed Kevin to think we didn't keep that commitment because of his death. We continue to live out the Scripture that tells us to *"bear with each other and forgive one another . . . as the Lord forgave you"* (Colossians 3:13, NIV). Easy? No! Worth it? Absolutely!

CHAPTER SIXTEEN

The Baggage of Loss

"If we are to travel happily, we must travel light."
—Angie Ford-Green

NO ONE TOLD ME HOW PAST LOSSES MIGHT piggyback on top of my grief over Kevin, or that it can be negatively cumulative and leave a lasting imprint on my subconscious mind. But the fact is unrealized, unexpressed, and unresolved loss, tangible or intangible, can cause someone who is grieving to be troubled by past losses. Probably the most troubling reality I had to accept was that grief is circular, ongoing, and never ends.

Everyone experiences loss during their lifetime. Sometimes it involves the death of a person, others are less traumatic than a death, but hurtful, nevertheless. It hurts to suffer the loss of a pet, moving away from all that is familiar, and leaving special relationships behind. The loss of a job, a house, the betrayal of someone once considered a friend, or challenges to our emotional, spiritual, or physical health are real too.

Children can experience loss at an early age, and the adults in their lives might not realize they sense and understand more than adults think they do. Like adults, children need someone to talk to them about what's happening. They also need permission to feel the hurt and the pain without grief consuming their little lives. Unfortunately, children are often not included at all in grieving or, to the other extreme, are brought into it much too deeply.

Adults who are grieving have an obligation to seek wise counsel that can help them to find a healthy balance concerning their children. Unless they understand and learn how to help children become acquainted with sorrow and loss, their unexpressed and unresolved grief from their younger years can be carried into their adult lives. The heaviness of that childhood grief can become like baggage they lug around until it is unpacked.

This was true for me. Until Kevin died, I was unaware of the baggage of loss from my past—not so much from loss and grief caused by death, but by disappointment, betrayal, regret, resentment, anger, and feelings my life wasn't quite what I'd hoped and dreamed it would be.

The emotions attached to those losses from my child-hood were deeply buried and needed my attention.

When I began unpacking, I was surprised at just how many past losses I had experienced as a girl, into my teens, and as a young adult. Too busy, easily distracted, and possessing the "get over it" attitude encouraged by our culture, I had never taken the time to stop and con-sider how those losses were affecting me and weighing me down. To do so seemed senseless and self-indulging.

Encouraged through personal counseling to take a look inside my baggage of loss, I discovered a great deal of sadness between the ages of four and nine years old connected to our family moving from Arkansas to Connecticut to upstate New York, then back to Connecticut, and to Arkansas, before our final move to California. With each move I had to leave my grandparents, who I was very close to, as well as family members, neighbors, playmates, school and church friends, and the places I had called home.

At 5 years old, we had moved from Arkansas to Connecticut. My first day of Kindergarten, I was asked by the teacher to stand up, say my name, and tell everyone where I was from. Unafraid, I boldly said, "Hi! My name is Angie. I'm from Arkansas!"

Laughter filled the room. No one had ever laughed at me that way. Did I look okay? Was there something wrong with me? As I sat down in my chair, the kids kept talking and giggling. After class, I asked the teacher why everyone laughed.

"It's because of your cute Southern accent," she answered.

I was confused. "What's an accent?" I asked.

"You come from a place where people talk differently than we do here in Connecticut. You are not from here, and the way you talk is cute, but different."

"Different" didn't sound like a good thing to me, and for the next few weeks, I only talked at school when I had to. Listening intently to how the other kids spoke, I couldn't tell that they sounded any different than I did. I decided maybe *they* were the ones who were different.

Being so young, I didn't understand the degree to which that experience had hurt, embarrassed, and caused me to mourn the loss of the people and places where I had once belonged. When I finally mentioned what had happened to my parents, they told me I was different—I was special—and they encouraged me to never change. That really helped me. At that age, I needed to feel like I belonged. Nevertheless, I made some adjustments to how I spoke and created a Southern, East Coast accent of my own, and no one can guess where I am originally from.

After Kevin died, when I realized I hadn't really grieved such previous losses in my life, including the death of my dad, I became aware of what I had been lugging around for far too long. Grief unrealized is grief unreleased, and that type of grief was affecting my emotional and physical health in negative ways. Past grief can make present grief all the more complicated. My baggage of loss was very heavy. If I had not unpacked it little by little, I doubt I would have healed or experienced the sense of peace I enjoy now.

Writing this book and learning about grief teaches me there will always be some unpacking to do. Loss will constantly be a part of life, and so will the need to grieve the losses experienced.

Are you carrying the baggage of loss? How heavy is your baggage? Are you ready to do some unpacking? I encourage you to open your baggage of loss. It is not a simple task, but there is much to be gained from lightening the load.

"Let us also lay aside every weight." (Hebrews 12:1, ESV)

CHAPTER SEVENTEEN

A Grateful Heart

"Give thanks to the LORD, for he is good; his love endures forever." (1 Chronicles 16:34, NIV)

WHEN I LOOK FOR WHAT IS GOOD AND WORTHY OF gratitude and praise, things change. I change, and God gets the glory because He is worthy. Doing a root word study on the word "glory," I found it means "happy" or "happiness." Learning this has altered my way of thinking about what it means to bring glory to God. Because I love Him, I want to make Him happy. It seems only natural to want to please my Heavenly Father. As a mother to my sons and MiMi to my grandchildren and great-grandchildren, they make me very happy.

Though I didn't, and still don't, understand why God took my son, He continues to convince me of His unfailing love and blessings. A "blessing" is defined as God's "protection and favor." Though it was difficult to count my blessings, and it didn't seem God had protected and showed His favor when Kevin died, His protection and favor after my son's death could not be ignored or denied. The reality is that it's very hard to feel protected and in God's favor when we are up to our necks in the turbulent and raging waters of grief pushing against us and dragging us down.

Once the initial flood of grief subsided, I made a list of the evidence proving how God was protecting and covering my family and me with His grace. Making this list was very helpful and once again opened the eyes of my heart.

- It was a blessing Kevin stopped by the house before he went surfing on his last day on earth, so we could spend a few precious minutes together.

- God's protection and grace covered Kevin at death because he died instantly of sudden cardiac arrest. The doctors said he would not have known what was happening or have experienced any pain, suffering, or fear. Here one second and gone the next—what a way to go!

- Kevin's friend, Todd, was surfing with him that morning. A professional lifeguard and experienced surfer, he was able to get Kevin out of the water, onto his board, and to the shore. Because of his training and knowledge, Todd knew Kevin was gone. If that had not been the case, Todd would have started life support.

- It was a blessing the kitchen phone started beeping a high-pitched alarm and the hospital was able to get in touch with me before I walked out the front door to go to work the morning Kevin died. If I had left a minute sooner, only God knows how long it would have taken for the hospital to get in touch with us. Bob and I didn't have cell phones.

- Our family members and close friends were at our side immediately. Our lifelong friends from Northern California came down within hours and stayed with us for a week. Another precious friend and her husband came from Arizona to be with us during the graveside and memorial services.

- My cousin and aunt from New Mexico arrived within 24 hours, and Bob and I didn't want them to leave. They were so loving and helped keep the house in some sort of order. I will always treasure the memories of my aunt sweeping the dirt off the courtyard from all the flowers and plants that were delivered, washing dishes by hand, and just being present to us. Having my cousin massage my neck and shoulders while praying over me was such a tender and tangible blessing.

- Our house looked like the inside of a lovely florist shop. The first floral gift to arrive was a huge (and I mean HUGE) orchid plant in a clay pot with no card. This anonymous gift was a show of extravagant love and beauty.

- Warm, freshly baked chocolate chip cookies, bagels, and bags of groceries were brought in person or delivered to us daily. These gifts of compassion, sympathy, and comfort added blessing upon blessing. We were surrounded, warmed, and strengthened by the love they represented.

- My great uncle, Faye, and his wife, Althea, gave us a casket for Kevin to be buried in, and personally drove it to us from Sacramento. (They were in their eighties.) Their gift saved us the heartache and expense of having to choose and purchase a casket, which was another act of extravagant love.

Our family experienced God's protection and grace every day. Though suffering, His presence and His love surrounded us and filled our home and lives.

My earliest memory of God's protection and grace came when I was five years old during a life-threatening hurricane in Connecticut. My dad, my mom, my baby brother, and I sat around our kitchen table with a kerosene lamp in the middle. It was the only light in the house—the power had been out for hours. The winds howled, and the windows throughout the house rattled and shook. I should have been terrified, but I wasn't. My dad was with us. There was nothing to be afraid of if he was with us—he was my hero and protector.

To turn our attention away from the storm, my dad spoke words of comfort, encouraging us to trust God. He led us in a prayer, thanking God for the kerosene lamp that lit up the darkness. He praised Him for being more powerful than the storm. My dad emphasized how God was the Light in all darkness and the Creator of the universe who was in control of the storm and the captain of our little ship. He also spoke over us the Bible passage that declares God is our *"refuge and strength, a very present help in trouble"* (Psalm 46:1, ESV). Our family was in trouble, and God was our protector.

My mom echoed Dad's prayer and added she was thankful for my dad's strong faith and trust in God. I added how I was thankful my dad had bought the kerosene lamp that gave us light. My little one-year-old brother was sitting in his high chair and couldn't express what he was thankful for, but I told God I was grateful for my sweet "Bubby" who I adored. Rusty smiled at me and brightened up the room. I am convinced he understood what I said.

With the storm raging through the night, we moved from the kitchen table to the living room couch. Huddled and cuddled up together, we sang songs, and my baby brother and I fell asleep and slept peacefully under the protective covering of our parents and God.

At dawn, the storm had passed, and we all went outside to see the damage and debris left in its path. Many of our neighbor's homes had roofs that were blown off or were severely damaged. Clotheslines, electrical poles, and fences were down. Our house and yard were relatively unchanged with only a few tree limbs scattered in the yard. We had a lot to be thankful for, and I've never forgotten that stormy night and how my parents led us in praise and worship in the midst of the storm.

One of my favorite stories about how to respond when dealing with the storms of life features two women walking together down a flight of stairs. Both suddenly fell, and when they got up, one complained, "Why did that happen? Things like this always happen to me. It's not fair!"

The other woman checked to make sure nothing was broken and said, "Whew! I'm glad that's over!" That is the woman I want to be—a woman of gratitude.

There are several what I call "life songs" that mean a lot to me and come to the surface in challenging times and seasons. One of those we sang at Kevin's memorial service, and it speaks of giving thanks with a grateful heart to the Holy One because He has given Jesus Christ, His Son. The lyrics proclaim how the weak are strong and the poor are rich because of what the LORD has done.

Giving thanks with a grateful heart while possessing an attitude of gratitude keeps me from becoming ungrateful and unable to see the blessings when I am weak and poor of spirit.

Psalms is considered to be one of the most popular books in the Bible with its theme and focus on praising God for His power and goodness. The following verses, along with so many others, encourage me to give thanks to Him in and out of the storms and sorrows of life.

"I will give thanks to the LORD with my whole heart: I will recount all of your wonderful deeds."   (Psalm 9:1, ESV)

"I keep my eyes always on the LORD. With Him at my right hand, I will not be shaken."   (Psalm 16:8, NIV)

"*The heavens declare the glory of God; the skies proclaim the work of His hands.*"   (Psalm 19:1, BSB)

"*LORD, my Rock and my Redeemer.*" (Psalm 19:14, NIV)

"*The LORD is my shepherd, I lack nothing.*" (Psalm 23:1, NIV)

"*Taste and see that the LORD is good; blessed is the one who takes refuge in him.*"   (Psalm 34:8, NIV)

"*The LORD is the light and my salvation—whom shall I fear? The LORD is the stronghold of my life—of whom shall I be afraid?*"   (Psalm 27:1, NIV)

"*Before the mountains were born or you brought forth the whole world, from everlasting to everlasting you are God.*"
          (Psalm 90:2, NIV)

"*My soul is weary with sorrow; strengthen me according to your word.*"   (Psalm 119:28, NIV)

CHAPTER EIGHTEEN
He Sings to Me

"The LORD your God . . . will rejoice over you with gladness; He will quiet you with His love; He will rejoice over you with singing." (Zephaniah 3:17, BSB)

DURING THE GOOD, THE BAD, AND THE UGLY OF MY life, God has used music to sing to me of His redeeming love. He is the song in my heart, and music is the language of my soul.

My mother was an accomplished musician with a lovely singing voice, an ear for music, and perfect pitch. She could hear a note played or sung and actually name the note. When she was in college, she was the student assistant director for one of her professors as well as for the Philharmonic orchestra in

Los Angeles. Needless to say, our home and everyday lives were filled with music.

With what my mom described as my "natural show-manship and stage presentation," she believed I was destined for stardom. She devoted hours singing to and with me. As my primary vocal coach, my mother taught me voice production as well as how to sight-read sheet music, sing on pitch so I was neither sharp or flat, and project my voice with or without a microphone. Though she encouraged me to "sell" a song," that wasn't me. All I wanted to do was sing. I never saw myself as a star. Just the thought of that reminds me of a funny memory when my high school English teacher, who was also the head of our drama club, told me, "You are definitely a star, but I have no idea where you might hang." His comment still makes me laugh out loud.

Stardom and fame never appealed to me. Simply lis-tening to and making music was what I enjoyed the most. While singing solos was not my favorite thing, I sang a lot of them at church, in school, at weddings, funerals, and special events. When we lived in Connecticut and I was in Kindergarten, the school principal said I had a "voice like an angel beyond my years," and asked if she could take me around to classes for a week to lead the singing of "America the Beautiful" and "God Bless America" to start off the school day. With so many unsolicited opportunities for making music, I thank God and my precious mom for bringing out the song in me.

Comfortable and self-confident singing became the heart and soul of who I was and what I did for more than 40 years. That's why I remember how sad and troubling it had been to hear my mom tell a friend, "The song is dead. The music is gone," after my dad died. I didn't understand what she meant until Kevin died. I couldn't sing a note without choking on tears, and I wasn't sure I would ever be able to really sing again.

Then I considered that when God formed me in my mother's womb (Psalm 139), He also created within me the song I have to sing, and His spirit often sings to me. Never has He sung such sweet music as He did after He took Kevin. The music in me didn't die. God's song remained alive within me, and He continues to give me a song to sing.

Since Kevin's death, I have written and published a new rendition of the Lord's Prayer and several light-hearted, whimsical children's songs that I, along with my Cunningham and Green book publishing coauthor and illustrator, Judy Cunningham, are turning into books for pre-K to third-grade children. I strongly believe that none of the songs or stories would have been written or published unless God sang to me as His way to keep music alive in my soul.

Some say there are muses who inspire creativity in artists. I believe there is sound, theological evidence in Zephaniah 3:17 that reveals God *is* the muse, but I also wonder how He actually goes about inspiring us. Do musically inclined angels bring songs from Heaven? When I think of King David singing hymns and psalms while tending the sheep as a young shepherd and as the King of Israel, I wonder how those songs were given to him. There's much mystery about how God moves and ministers to His people. When I someday get to Heaven, I will finally understand more about Him and His ways. Until then, I know without a doubt that God gives the song.

After Kevin died, it took about a month before Bob and I could go back to church. It wasn't that we didn't want or need to be in the company of our church family. It was because we knew it was going to be emotional. We didn't want to weep all over ourselves in public. Then, one Sunday in church, we were singing one of my favorite praise songs. With my eyes closed and tears pouring out of my eyes, down my cheeks, and off my face, my hands reached out for God in adoration and praise. I felt warm all over. In that moment, I had an overwhelming sense that Kevin was worshipping and praising God in that moment. Somehow, we were standing together in a holy and sacred space. Tears of grief became tears of joy, and my connection to God and my son was profoundly real. We were joined together then because of the love and Spirit of God that binds us together forever. We were in one accord and of one spirit.

That Sunday morning, I sang with a voice clear and strong—and the music goes on.

"You turned my wailing into dancing; you removed my sackcloth and clothed me with joy, that my heart may sing your praises and not be silent. LORD my God, I will praise you forever." (Psalm 30:11–12, NIV)

"I will sing to the LORD as long as I live; I will sing praise to my God while I have being." (Psalm 104:33, ESV)

"Because you are my help, I will sing in the shadow of your wings." (Psalm 63:7, NIV)

"Sing, all you who ware upright in heart!" (Psalm 32:11, NIV)

"The brook would lose its song if God removed the rocks." —Unknown

CHAPTER NINETEEN

Comfort and Healing

"Blessed are those who mourn, for they shall be comforted."
(Matthew 5:4, ESV)

TO HEAL IS A VERB, AND ITS DEFINITION IS TO
"make sound or whole . . . to be restored to health;
to restore to original purity or integrity; to return to a
sound state" (*Webster's Dictionary*).

When in survival mode, there were times I wondered if I would survive the pain and sorrow of the
loss and grief I was experiencing. From the beginning
of my journey through grief, God called me to draw
close to Him.

To rest in Him. To trust Him.

To lean into Him and claim His promises as my own.

Because of my faith and previous experiences with Him in other trials and heartbreaking situations, I chose Him as the One who would comfort, strengthen, and heal me.

My first step toward healing was to connect my hurt to the Healer. My next step was to give myself permission to grieve. The book, *Understanding Your Grief: Ten Essential Touchstones for Finding Hope and Healing Your Heart*, by Dr. Alan D. Wolfelt, was very helpful. In it, he introduces the "Six Needs of Mourning" as an essential guide for better understanding what is important and needed in grieving.

1. Acknowledge the reality of the death.
2. Embrace the pain of the loss.
3. Remember the person who died.
4. Develop a new self-identity.
5. Search for meaning.
6. Let others help you—now and always.

Though these needs do not have to be addressed in chronological order, Dr. Wolfelt suggests we seriously consider "yielding" to them.

In my grieving, I immediately acknowledged and accepted the reality of Kevin's death. I had no sense of denial. Embracing the pain and remembering Kevin was easy—they went hand in hand. As I gave myself permission to grieve any place and any time, from the very first day of my loss, I searched for meaning and purpose by going to God's Word that is, and will always be, the *"lamp unto my feet, and a light unto my path"* (Psalm 119:105, KJV). Still, while remembering Kevin came naturally, asking for help did not. But, when I finally did ask, it was of real value. The idea of developing a new self-identity seemed absurd for quite a while. How could I be someone different when Kevin had been such a significant part of who I was?

Connecting with other moms through Umbrella Ministries, a Christian-based support ministry for grieving mothers, helped me to know I wasn't alone in my loss and to consider I wasn't the only woman in the world to ever suffer the death of a child. Spending quality time with other grieving moms in a welcoming, accepting, and safe place allowed me to express my grief openly and honestly and open my heart to others who were hurting and grieving like I was. Being in the company of other women of faith was a very comforting, encouraging, and strengthening connection.

Over time, I realized I was changing and during those times I asked myself and the LORD several questions.

"Will I always think of myself as a grieving mom?'

What matters most to me now?

"Do I accept that I am different?"

"What do I want to change? What do I want to stay the same?"

One thing I knew for sure was that I would not miss anymore opportunities, make excuses, feel guilty, have regrets, make compromises or procrastinate. I didn't want to miss out on a nanosecond of life. My passion and joy for living took a while, but were eventually supercharged and my inner-world is in order.

Respectfully, I would like to add a seventh need to Dr. Wolfelt's list: prayer. Studies, and my life experiences, prove prayer helps in healing. For more than a year after Kevin died, my prayers were lists of what I thought God should do for me, my husband, and my family. Mostly, they were lamentations and petitions for relief as I pleaded and urged God to take away the grief and be the miracle in me, my marriage, and other relationships.

Until January 10, 2002, my prayers were expressions of love, gratitude, worship and intercessions for others. One Sunday in church, the pastor said, "God wants to meet your deepest need." As I looked around the sanctuary I could identify countless needs of others, but not any of my own. Suffering the loss of my son, from that day forward I began to consider that I, too, had needs that God wanted to meet, and I experienced the purpose and power of a more authentic prayer life. I also developed many other everyday habits and routines that proved helpful and healing.

Sun and fresh air became powerful symbols of life.

I took long walks in locations where I could enjoy God's creation.

Having coffee early in the morning on our patio, listening to birdsongs and the trickle of our water fountain soothed my suffering spirit.

Leaving the house to drive along the beach and stop for a latte or tasty treat were things I hadn't done in the past.

A high-spirited extrovert, I learned to be still.

I learned how to take time for personal inventory and self-awareness,

Physical touch became more important to me. Affection displayed and shared was most comforting.

Some who grieve might overeat or use alcohol or prescription drugs in an attempt to ease their pain. Food didn't matter much to me, and though I tried drinking alcohol socially for a short time, it was obvious to me that wasn't going to help.

Grief can override our ability to realize we are thirsty, and dehydration can compound feelings of fatigue and disorientation. I avoided caffeinated beverages and drank more water and herbal teas.

Able to sleep interrupted before Kevin died, I suddenly had trouble sleeping. I came across an article in a magazine about the effects of sleep deprivation and I took the advice of the doctor who wrote the article to establish a consistent bedtime routine. I also bought (and continue to replace and refresh) new bedding, spraying lavender and linen scents on sheets and pillows.

The work of grief is exhausting and from time to time I had to take a break and do something I referred to as grief relief. Shopping became a distraction and a temporary fix. Gardening and digging around in the good earth was cathartic and introduced me to the joy of gardening that has now become a significant part of my life.

I learned how to say "no" when asked to help with a project or attend a social event. Saying "yes" only when it felt right.

Visiting a bookstore, flower, sculpture garden, or art gallery keeps me connected to some of my happy places.

Walking along a seashore picking up shells and looking for sea glass became one of my favorite pastimes.

Getting away helped Bob and me to see things from a different perspective. We made weekend trips to Palm Springs. We visited friends and family in other places. We would just get in our car and drive, not knowing where we were going until we were on the road. For more than a year, Bob and I visited Kevin's grave at least once a week. While this kept the harsh reality of his death at the forefront, it was also a healing ritual in a sacred, holy place that we needed.

The times I was most comfortable and experienced the deepest levels of healing and peace were when

I imagined the LORD with me. I spent several hours leaning into Him, allowing Him to hold and comfort me. The time with the Healer was medicine to my grief-sick heart, soul, mind, and body.

As I began to heal and recover from the shock of Kevin's death, life seemed to get back to some sense of normal again, and I made a list of the evidence.

- I am not weeping uncontrollably every day.
- I am not marking time according to the day Kevin died.
- I don't feel like I'm going to die.
- I don't want to die.
- I am glad to be alive
- I don't feel like I'm going crazy.
- I'm not living life in slow motion anymore.
- I am sleeping through the night.
- I can think about someone or something other than Kevin.
- I am able to appreciate simple pleasures.
- I am not tense and restless all the time.
- I am smiling more.
- I am laughing a little.
- I am singing again.
- I have joy.
- I have hope for the future.

After completing my list, I saw there was hope for better days ahead. I realized there would always be moments when I would wish things could have been different. Kevin and Venus could have been married with children, living their best lives together. When Kevin died, so did the dreams and plans he had for his life with Venus. Everyone in our family loved Vee and were glad she was going to be a "Green." She eventually married, had a son and daughter, but that relationship ended badly after a few short years. We all want to see her happy and with someone who will love and cherish her as much as Kevin did. I pray that special person will come into her life and stay.

As I daily walk in God's love and grace, I continue to experience healing and peace. God has revealed His love and goodness to me in profound and extravagant ways, and I believe His Word when He says, *"My grace is sufficient for you, for my power is made perfect in weakness . . . For when I am weak, then I am strong"* (2 Corinthians 12:9–10, NIV).

There is so much to be grateful for, and hopefully, no matter what I experience in the future, I will always give thanks to Him with a grateful heart.

"For I know the plans I have for you, declares the LORD, plans to prosper you and not to harm you, to give you a future and a hope."   (Jeremiah 29:11, BSB)

CHAPTER TWENTY

Heart to Heart

"Rejoice with those who rejoice, weep with those who weep."
(Romans 12:15, ESV)

AT WHAT SEEMED JUST THE RIGHT TIME, Bob and I decided to attend an introductory session of a new grief support group at our church. We were in trouble as a couple, and we knew it. We thought getting together with others who were grieving would somehow help. Unfortunately, the session was awkward for both of us. It was not specifically tailored to those who had experienced the loss of a child, so we found it difficult to relate to the grief being shared. I had thoughts like, *It's normal for aging parents to die. You are blessed you had your parents so long. Our son died at 28 years old,* or, *It's sad to lose a brother, a sister, or a friend, but to lose a child is much different!*

Watching Bob squirm in his chair told me he must have been thinking the same thing.

The guilt I felt about not relating, much less caring about other people's loss and grief, troubled me. Normally, I was empathetic and more concerned about others. But my emotions were raw, and I needed to hear from someone who had suffered the same kind of loss I had. Toward the end of the session, a woman shared about the loss of her only son who had died of suicide at the stroke of midnight on New Year's Eve, 2000. Bob leaned forward to listen to her, and I hung on every word she shared. Finally, here was someone who understood our pain!

After the meeting, she introduced herself. "Hello. My name is Cynthia. I am very sorry to learn of the loss of your son, Kevin." She then asked for my phone number. "We should get together and stay in touch," she said.

During one of our many phone conversations, Cynthia invited me to go with her to a retreat for grieving moms hosted by the Christian grief-support ministry I mentioned earlier, Umbrella Ministries, based in Palm Springs. Scheduled for the weekend before Mother's Day, I was skeptical. "What good can come from being with a lot of grieving moms?" I asked.

"Yes, the moms are grieving like we are, but they are grieving with hope," Cynthia replied. "Please come with me. This is a very special group of women I'd like you to meet."

Bob encouraged me to go, telling me if it was too painful or uncomfortable, he would drive to Palm Springs to pick me up at any hour of the day or night. I decided to go and Cynthia and I drove there together. When we arrived at the hotel, I didn't want to get out of the car. Sensing my hesitation, Cynthia said, "One step at a time. Let's check in."

Entering the lobby of the hotel triggered mixed feelings. It was five months since Kevin died. *What was I doing in Palm Springs where Bob and I had come many times for fun? Now, I'm going to spend a weekend with grieving moms. What was I thinking when I agreed to this?* Standing in line to check in, Cynthia put her hand on my arm and said, "It will be okay. Just breathe."

Walking through the lobby, and in the elevator on the way to our room, Cynthia greeted women she knew with smiles and hugs. Each time she greeted someone new, it made me feel more alone than I already felt. I knew no one. I barely knew Cynthia. I felt like a foreigner in a foreign land. I wanted out of there! Before Kevin died, staying in a hotel in Palm Springs was something different that I thoroughly enjoyed, and I always met new people while spending time at the pool. Before Kevin died, I enjoyed people. This was no longer true, and the thought of meeting grieving moms actually made me wince, and I felt sick to my stomach. I was afraid. *What if I couldn't relate to people anymore? What if that friendly, outgoing me was gone?*

Cynthia had told me we were rooming with a young mom who had suffered the loss of her teenage son six months before, and I expected her to be hurting as much as I was. When we entered the room, she greeted us with a smile, and, unlike me, she did not look like a drowned cat. Getting acquainted, she talked about her son and her grief openly, honestly, and easily. Why was she at the retreat? It didn't seem she needed to be there at all.

"Why are you here this weekend?" I asked.

"I want to be with other moms like me," she replied. Her response puzzled me, making me wonder again why I had chosen to come.

Our next step was to attend a meet-and-greet session. As I entered the room, it was very disturbing to see the large number of mothers who had gathered and were milling around. The conference room could accommodate more than a hundred people, and it was filled to capacity. I was ready to call Bob to come and take me home. *I don't want to be a part of this group,* I thought.

Cynthia put her hand on my arm. "Come on. Let's do this together," she said.

In the pre-registration packet, we had been encouraged to bring a picture of the child we lost to place on a photo gallery board titled "We Will Remember You." Standing in line to place the picture of Kevin on the board, I couldn't move forward when it was my turn. My hands shook, and I fought back tears. As I backed away, I bumped against the arms of an elderly woman.

"Hello, dear. May I see your picture?"

I couldn't hand it to her. She gently repeated, "May I see?"

Reluctantly, I let go of the photo.

"Is this your son? He's so handsome. What is his name?"

It surprised me she didn't use the past tense. Everyone else before had said, "He *was* so handsome." Somehow, that empowered me to speak.

"That's my son, Kevin," I replied, almost in a whisper. "He died of sudden cardiac death while surfing."

"He's so handsome," the woman replied, once more in present tense. "I'm so sorry for your loss, and I'm glad you are here this weekend. Do you want me to place Kevin's picture on the board next to my son, Jonathon?" she asked.

In her other hand was a picture of Jonathon, and she handed it to me as she held on to Kevin's picture.

"He died of cancer two years ago," she said. "I had him late in life after three miscarriages. He is my miracle child."

Tears filled my eyes, not for myself, but for this precious mother like me.

Until I met Cynthia, our young roommate, and that precious woman, it seemed I was the only woman in the world who had suffered and was living with the loss of a child. My son. My loss. My grief was all that seemed to matter to me.

In that defining moment, I knew that was why I was at the retreat—to meet other mothers like me.

One of the keynote speakers, Susan Perez, was a vivacious young mom from Texas who had suffered the loss of her dad, her son, and her daughter in a train accident the year before Kevin died. Susan laid out her grieving heart before us while emphasizing the faith and hope that sustained her, the assurance from God's gift of eternal life that someday she and the family she had lost would be together again. It was obvious she was a woman of faith because of what Jesus has done to give all who believe in Him everlasting life. I hoped I would one day be where she was in her journey of grief, as she kept encouraging us to give ourselves permission to grieve, while holding on to hope.

In my grieving, I had faith and hope, but I wasn't sure how long it would take for me to be where Susan was just a year after such a devastating loss.

Connecting with Umbrella Ministries, helped me to know I wasn't alone in my loss and to consider I wasn't the only woman in the world to ever suffer the death and loss of a child. Spending quality time with other moms in a welcoming, accepting, and safe place allowed me to express my grief openly and honestly, and I opened my heart to others who were hurting and grieving too.

CHAPTER TWENTY-ONE

Who Am I Now?

"My days are like the evening shadow; I wither away like grass."
(Psalm 102:11, NLT)

IF YOU ASKED ANY MOTHER WHO HAS SUFFERED the loss of a child at any age and cause, they would tell you the journey through grief changes who they are. This is surely true for me. There were many times through the years when I wasn't sure who I was, and that I might never find my true self again.

Though Kevin wasn't very good about giving cards and gifts on Mother's Day, he gave me the best gift he could have ever given when he wrote a poem for me the Mother's Day before he died. The words of this poem helped to remind me who I was, and how he saw me, which helped me to find myself again.

My Beautiful Mother

You are a lady whom I'm proud to say
I've grown to love more every day.
You have always been there willing and waiting.
You have always cared and put your children first.
So, now I'm older and can plainly see
Just how good you've been to me.

Yes, you are like no other.
I'm talking about you, My Beautiful Mother.

I'm sorry for those who can't remember
Christmases spent with you in the month of December.

I still look back at what I miss.
So many things you healed with just a kiss.
I close my eyes and desperately relive the past,
Only to find out that it couldn't last.

Yes, you are like no other.
I'm talking about you, My Beautiful Mother.

I can picture you alone high atop a mountain
With the look of love surrounding you for Eternity.

Mom, I love you in every way.

Have a Happy Mother's Day.
For you are like no other.
I can only be talking about you.
My Beautiful Mother.

The line in the poem saying, "I can picture you alone high atop a mountain with the look of love surrounding you for Eternity" troubled me the first time I read it. I wondered what Kevin was telling me. He knew I am not someone who imagines myself in lofty places, and I have always been afraid of heights. No one would ever catch me climbing to the top of a mountain, much less a high one—no way, no how! For my son to picture me in this way assured me he knew I loved God and had experienced His love for me. This line also revealed his understanding and belief about Eternity. He imagined me surrounded by God's love, just as I imagine him now.

From the time we are very young until the end of our lives, it seems we all ask the same questions—Who am I? Where do I belong? What am I supposed to do? For me the answer is found in God's Word, and so the question of Who am I? is settled for me. How about you?

"Yet, to all who receive Him, to those who believed in His name, He gave the right to become children of God."

(John 1:12, NIV)

CHAPTER TWENTY-TWO

Mothers Like Me

"He comforts us in all our troubles so that we can comfort others. When they are troubled, we will be able to give them the same comfort God has given us."

(2 Corinthians 1:4, NLT)

AFTER TWO YEARS OF DISCUSSING, ENVISIONING, and praying about the possibility of creating and introducing a grief care and support ministry for moms, Cynthia Weightman (the mom I met at our church support group) and I cofounded Mothers Like Me Grief Care and Support Ministry that was introduced through my home church, Seacoast Grace, in March 2006.

The purpose of our ministry was to provide a welcoming, accepting, and safe place for hurting moms to come together to share their stories of loss, talk about their children, and express their grief. We also wanted to encourage them to draw close to God with our hope for them to receive His comfort, healing, and peace. Our ministry vision statement was to create a community and network of moms who would comfort others as they had been comforted.

We offered support groups, workshops, and other opportunities for moms to come together with other mothers acquainted with grief. We focused on helping our moms become aware of how grief affects our hearts, souls, minds, and bodies. We were intentional about providing helpful information and grief-related resources that would help them navigate through their grief, and we encouraged them to search for meaning and purpose in their loss.

Remembering and celebrating our children was a significant part of our ministry, especially on the child's birthday and during the holidays. Our hopeful prayer was that they would ultimately connect their hurt to the Healer, Jesus, and that they would not be crippled by their grief. One of the mothers who joined our first support group was Jewish. Though she was not interested in learning anything about Jesus, the Messiah, she wasn't offended if and when we spoke of Him. After one of the gatherings, she shared how she had never before experienced "love and acceptance in a group" as she did when she was with us. She said such love and acceptance was not normal to her, and we had encouraged her to open her heart to God after many years of turning away from her Jewish roots.

Through the years since then, I have learned mothers who were an active part of our ministry say we were their "lifeline" and the time spent with them made a positive and significant difference in their journey through grief. The bond we formed was heart-to-heart and soul-to-soul. It has been a blessing to also learn that many in the original group have gone on to comfort other moms as they were comforted.

After Bob retired in 2007, we seriously considered moving from California. We traveled to Arizona, Nevada, Oregon, and the Carolinas. I thought maybe I'd like to return to the South or the East Coast. We also visited Bob's cousins in Colorado and felt very comfortable in the college town of Fort Collins, nestled in the upper northernmost part of Colorado.

Leaving my aging mom, our sons and their families, other family members, lifelong friends, our home church, Kevin's grave, and the place we had lived for more than 50 years seemed bizarre to us as well as to some of those who were closest to us. Everyone was supportive and agreed we should do what we felt was best for us as a couple. Bob and I wondered if putting 1,100 miles between us and the life we had known for more than 50 years would be what was best for us, but we both sensed we needed a change.

I also sensed God was calling us to come away with Him.

As we contemplated the move, some of the women in our Mothers Like Me group expressed feelings of abandonment that weighed heavily on my heart. They didn't want me to leave, but after spending over a year with most of them, I wondered if maybe it was time for them to get back into the mainstream of life. As I prayed about the possible move, the words "help more moms in more places" kept running through my mind.

One day, Bob and I were stuck in traffic on one of the main freeways we had used for years. As I looked at the people in the cars around us in what was more like a parking lot than a flowing highway, I noticed how stressed and angry everyone appeared.

"Let's do it!" I declared to Bob. "Let's get out of here! We need a change. We need an adventure. We need something different."

We put our house on the market, and it sold after one open house. We made an offer on a house in Fort Collins, Colorado. Both escrows closed in 12 days. Talk about a quick launch! There was no time for "dilly-dal-lying," as my grandmother would've said, and certainly no time to change our minds. There was no turning back. We started packing.

One morning, I heard Bob sobbing in the attic. He had come across some of Kevin's things that were stored there. When he brought down the items, we both cried over a painting a friend had done for our son, a worn-out wetsuit Kevin had worn as a teen, and a skim board he had made himself.

We had forgotten about every one of those things. Did that mean we would forget about Kevin too?

A few days later, we called our sons and their wives to pick up patio furniture and other household items we wouldn't be taking with us. The looks on their faces told us our move was going to be hard on them, but no one said a word. They just encouraged us, as is their nature, respecting our decision. Several of their childhood friends stopped by to take a last look around the house they had spent a lot of time in; a few of them had briefly lived with us. For some reason I wasn't emotional about the move, and I wondered if once again I was in shock and just numb.

All of the visits and goodbyes tugged at my heart, and in those moments I had doubts about our decision. We had a very large community of family and friends in California. Our roots there were deep. We only knew four people in Colorado, and there wasn't an ocean or beach there. "We're not mountain people," I said to Bob. "What are we doing?"

Everything happened so fast we didn't have time to think, but that was probably a good thing. Closing the front door for the last time on the house we had called home for more than 30 years was harder than expected. Though it was never my dream house, it had been the place where we raised our boys, and it was a home filled with life, laughter, lots of love, and memories. We could only hope what was ahead would prove our decision to move was part of God's plan for our lives for good. We believed we needed a new start in a new place.

"A Song of Ascents. I will lift up my eyes to the hills— From whence comes my help?" (Psalm 121:1, KJV)

CHAPTER TWENTY-THREE

Helping More Moms
in More Places

*"Let each one of us [make it a practice to] please his neighbor
for his good, to build him up spiritually."*

(Romans 15:2, AMP)

WE MOVED INTO OUR NEW HOME IN FORT COLLINS,
Colorado, on January 9, 2008. In February, Bob and I went
to a couples Valentine's Day dinner at the church we were
attending. A woman sitting next to me introduced herself
as the director of women's ministry, and we got acquainted.
She was a straightforward woman and I liked her right away.
During our conversation, she asked if I had a heart for ministry. When I told her about Mothers Like Me, she said, "I
have five moms who need you right now."

Though I wasn't sure I was ready to begin the ministry so soon after our move, I thought of those five moms and agreed to help them. Barbara and the lead pastor of the church introduced the ministry to the congregation. A local newspaper did an article about parents who had suffered the loss of a child (there seemed to be an epidemic in the area). I was interviewed and information about Mothers Like Me was included in the article, which provided visibility and introduced the ministry to the Northern Colorado community.

My first grief care and support group met with eight moms in a five-week Grieving with Hope session. The women in that group were open, honest, and eager to express their grief and reach for hope and peace. The ministry grew in the number of moms who participated and the variety of opportunities for fellowship and friendship. As the size of the group increased, I invited some of the moms further along in their grief to join my ministry team and they accepted my invitation.

Together we comforted and encouraged moms suffering the loss of children of all ages, and varied and heart-wrenching causes of death—drug overdose, suicide, auto accident, cancer, and stillborn and infant deaths.

One especially troubling death for me was a nine-year-old girl struck and killed by a woman texting on her cell phone, only 15 peddles on her bike from home. That girl's young mom became a significant part of Mothers Like Me as assistant director. She also went on to be an important reason Colorado has a no texting while driving law. That courageous and hopeful mom will always be one of my heroes of hope!

In 2009, I was diagnosed with advanced and aggressive breast cancer. After five surgeries and subsequent cancer treatments, I had to step back and away from full-time grief ministry. It was a very difficult decision for me to lay aside the ministry I had settled on as one I would fulfill for the rest of my life. I had to hear from God to make sure it was time for me to walk away.

My oncologist—and my husband, Bob—encouraged me to make my health a priority, as did our sons and the rest of our family and friends. I believed that was God's encouragement as well. Though no one assumed my leadership responsibilities, there was a network of moms in place who I believed would companion with "more moms in more places." They did, and they still do!

After recovering from cancer, I continued to blog regularly, maintain a website for grieving moms and I have been a keynote speaker on the topic of grieving with hope. In May 2018, I was the featured speaker at a Hearts of Hope retreat for grieving moms in Connecticut, hosted by Helga Findley and her friend Ann Starke. Helga was the woman I met poolside at the Umbrella Ministries retreat in 2002.

When Helga and Ann invited me to speak, I didn't hesitate to say, "Yes! Of course I will!" I was also anxious to see Helga again and to meet Ann. My husband, Bob, and my brother, Russ, planned to meet me in Connecticut after the retreat for a sentimental journey. Russ was born in New London, Connecticut, and I had some wonderful memories of a place I called *one of my favorite homes.* Imagine my heartbreak and anxiety about speaking at the retreat in May when my precious brother, Russ, died of cancer in March.

Once again I cried out to God, "Why couldn't we have had our special trip together? I don't understand what You are doing. I trust You, but I can't always understand Your timing and Your ways."

Helga and Ann were loving, understanding, and supportive. They gave me the safe space I needed to grieve while encouraging me to use my grief to connect with grieving moms at the retreat. "Just be you. Share what's on your heart with the focus on how you grieved the loss of Kevin—and now Russ—with hope," Helga said. Because my heart was hurting, bruised, and tender from the loss of my brother, it was easy to connect with the hurts of the moms because I was experiencing fresh grief.

The retreat site was beautiful, a setting along the Eastern Seaboard at Manchester, Connecticut. Spending time in Connecticut for a week was like a homecoming.

Everything felt familiar. I was surprised I could find my way driving around the city of Groton, where we had lived when I was five to seven years old. And I met a cousin I had never met who was named after my dad.

Timothy Paul and I shared a delightful day at the harbor in New London. He told me things about our grandparents and my dad's family I never knew. Tim was warm and real, and he made me laugh. His sense of humor reminded me of my brother, Russ, which was comforting.

The day with Tim and the week in Connecticut were just what I needed after the death of my precious brother. From the assessments by the moms at the retreat, it was what they needed too. God's timing was perfect. His timing is always perfect! Why do I ever question His timing? His ways? I guess I'm just a slow learner.

Comforting and encouraging hurting moms was the most impactful ministry of my life. God brought hundreds of moms who allowed me to enter into their grief, trusting me, but there is one mother I am still concerned about. She only came to one support group gathering. As she shared about the loss of her daughter, I was sure she was very new in her loss. When I asked her how long it had been, she said, "It's been forty years." The other moms in the group gasped, and I said, "It sounds like it still feels like yesterday for you."

Her reply was, "Yes. It's just like that, and time doesn't heal."

Crippled by and stuck in her grief, time hadn't healed that hurting mom, and she was right. Time doesn't heal. Time can actually make things worse if one grieves without hope and gets stuck, unable to move out of the shadows of death. Sadly, I never saw or heard from that mom again, and I think it was because there was too much hope in the group of moms. She was grieving without hope. How I hope and pray she experienced God's love and healing touch at some point in her season of grief.

Every mother's face, name, and the names of their children are imprinted on my heart, as are their stories of loss, grief, and healing. I will be forever bonded to my sisters of the heart. For me a bond is a heart-to-heart, soul-to-soul connection that cannot be broken. The bond I share with other "moms like me" is a bond tied together by God's heartstrings. Another "three-stranded cord not easily broken."

If you are reading this book and you are one of the precious moms who God brought my way, I want you to know I will always remember you, and I thank God for YOU!

"May the LORD smile upon you and be gracious to you."
(Numbers 6:25, NLT)

CHAPTER TWENTY-FOUR

The In-Between

"The important thing to you is not how many years in your life, but how much life is in your years." —Unknown

AT THE END OF MY LIFE I WILL PROBABLY ASK MYSELF, "Did I live a good life? Did I love well? Was I loved? Did my life make a difference to anyone?

It seems to me life is made up of opposites like love/hate, ups/downs, highs/lows, strengths/weaknesses, success/failure, positive/negative, joy/sorrow, storms/calm weather, hope/hopelessness, belief/disbelief, truth/fiction, war/peace, lost/found, and life/death. Highs and lows, loving or not loving, being weak or strong, experiencing success or failure, and looking at the glass half-empty or half-full are all a normal part of life.

On Kevin's headstone are the dates of his birth and death with a dash in-between. This is true of most headstones in cemeteries. The announcement of when the person arrived and departed from this life marks their existence. Kevin wanted the world to know he was here.

When we had a new concrete driveway poured, he wrote his name in the wet cement. When a new concrete patio was poured in the backyard, he imprinted his eight-year-old hand, and wrote "The Greens," and the date in the wet cement.

After he died, Bob and I were taking a walk in our neighborhood, and we came across another place where Kevin wrote his name in wet cement. On another walk, we found the word *Verde*—Spanish for green, etched in cement. Bob and I had no idea he had gone throughout our neighborhood writing his name in what would become stone. We would not be surprised to find more of his markings. He left his mark on our family, his friends, the neighborhood, his hometown, and the world around him.

Standing over Kevin's grave and seeing his name and dates of birth and death etched in the headstone for the first time drew my attention to the dash between the dates. That little dash marked 28 years of his life. It seemed a poor representation of those years.

One afternoon I walked around the section of the cemetery where we had laid our son's body to rest. As I walked, I read the headstones of others laid to rest. Some of the dashes marked a life of a baby who was born and died on the same day. Some marked the life of a teenager, most of elderly people who had lived as many as 90 years. Each life marked. Each life remembered. That afternoon made me very aware of the dash, and it was important for me to make my dash count. What would that dash say about me? What will your dash say about you? What do you want it to say?

For Kevin, the dash represents a life filled with love, laughter, playing, surfing, fun, faith, and close—very close—family ties, as well as lifelong friendships. In his short 28 years, he made a lasting difference for everyone he knew. He connected and engaged naturally with all types of people. He was deeply loved and appreciated. He was authentic. He "seized the day," as he would say. He was unforgettable. His death was unthinkable, and I wondered if I would ever truly live again.

To Bob's and my amazement, we have lived a LOT of life since our son left this world in 2002.

We have cried.

We have laughed.

My husband and family survived my menopause (a true miracle).

We have traveled.

We retired from full-time employment.

We relocated to Colorado.

I survived breast cancer.

We welcomed our grandson, Kevin (he's named after Uncle Kevin).

We celebrated our 50th high school reunion.

We celebrated our 50th wedding anniversary.

My brother, Russ, died of cancer.

Bob's brother had to move into assisted living.

My mother had to move into a long-term care facility.

My mother died in 2021.

All of our granddaughters are married with children.

And—I need a drum roll please—I caught my first fish. It was the size of bait, but to me it was like an orca whale.

I am a published songwriter and coauthor of quality children's books.

Bob and I will turn 76 years old this year—and we look it—but don't feel it.

Our marriage is strong, and we love each other more than ever.

We are healed from the deep wounds and heartache of loss.

We live in peace and harmony.

We are content.

We have a lot to celebrate and to be thankful for—a completely different outcome than we would have expected during our time spent in the wilderness and trenches of grief.

Now very much aware of the dash between the dates of my life, I want that dash to represent a life well-lived with faith, hope, and love. We all write the story that fills in the dash. I want to carve my name on hearts, etching the stories I share now and in the future.

"The greatest legacy one can pass on to one's children and grandchildren is not money or other material things accumulated in one's life, but rather the legacy of character and faith." —Billy Graham

CHAPTER TWENTY-FIVE

At the Edge of Eternity

"He has made everything beautiful in its time. He has also set eternity in the human heart; yet no one can fathom what God has done from beginning to end."

(Ecclesiastes 3:11, NIV)

I BELIEVE DEATH TAKES THE BODY, AND GOD TAKES the soul; our invisible, infinite, eternal self. I also believe our souls long for eternity, for what will last, as we live in a world where "Nothing lasts forever. Nothing stays the same" (Donnelly Fenn, 2011).

Since I was a young child, my heart's longing has been to be a significant and active part of God's Kingdom *"on earth as it is in Heaven"* (Matthew 6:10, NIV), to be aligned with God's will and purpose. To love, honor, trust, and obey Him, and to know when I die, I will be welcomed into Heaven, because of the gift of eternal life given through the death and resurrection of Jesus Christ, His Son (John 3:16).

Just the thought of stepping into Heaven where there will be no more tears, sorrow, pain, wickedness, evil and sin, no more wars, and no more goodbyes brings me much hope and peace. Because of my belief and faith in God, I am not afraid to die knowing where and to whom I am going.

After the death of our son, Kevin, eternity became much clearer and closer to me, and I recall something of what C. S. Lewis wrote about better understanding the shift in my perspective and attachment to this life, because I was made for another world. My journey through grief set me on a path of sorrow and pain, but also on a path that led me to catching a glimpse of Heaven, and I now live at the edge of eternity.

The loss of Kevin tested and refined me like nothing before or since. At one point in the refining fire, I considered how confident I was Kevin was with God, and that when I die I will be reunited with my son, and all those I have loved who have gone on before me. The following questions are just some of what I needed to ask myself.

What do I hope for and believe about life after death?
What do I know about Heaven?

Is there evidence Heaven is real?

Do I believe Kevin is in Heaven?

Do I believe I will go to Heaven after I die?

What assures me Heaven will be my eternal home and final destination?

As usual, God's Word was the *"lamp unto my feet, and a light unto my path"* (Psalm 119:105, KJV), and it was very clear to me that being a resident and citizen of Heaven is all about Jesus. He is *"the way, the truth and the life"* (John 14:6, ESV). Because I believe this to be true, I have confidence that I am redeemed, saved, and sealed with Him for all eternity. *"For God so loved the world that He gave His one and only Son, that whoever believes in Him shall not perish, but have eternal life. For God did not send His Son into the world to condemn the world, but to save the world through Him"* (John 3:16–17, NIV).

When I leave this earth, because of my belief in God's love and promise of resurrection and eternal life through Jesus, I will be launched into Heaven in the blink of an eye. Because I have spent my fair share of time in the valley of shadows, and at the edge of the grave, death is closer than we think, as is eternity.

It has also been my personal experience that because I allow God to determine and manage the course of my life, He always creates "beauty from ashes," and there's always hope for a new beginning. A better tomorrow. I have been covered, protected, influenced, and changed by nothing other than God's great love that constantly turns my heart and my attention toward Him and eternity. Better for the wear and tears of loss, grief, and suffering, I now better relate to the sufferings of Christ for my sake. God has also been faithful and *"enlarged me when I was in distress"* (Psalm 4:1, KJV). He did not keep me free *from* suffering, He has been with me *through* the suffering.

The suffering and sorrow I have experienced has been the change agent by which iron has entered my soul. For this infusion of iron, I thank the Ironmaker. Hopeful, resilient, staying on course and in my lane, I'm heading for the finish line and want to finish well. The idea of staying in my lane reminds me of a story my daughter-in-law shared about a Special Olympics event she helped to coordinate several years ago. The Special Olympics Committee determined the person who would win the gold medal would not be the one who ran the fastest or arrived at the finish line first. The winner would be the one who put one foot in front of the other, staying in their lane.

The lane God has set before me is marked by His love, presence in my life, and His loving movements and actions. It makes my life much more manageable to know the best way for me to live day-by-day is to stay in my lane, that sacred pathway that will lead me to my final destination. I believe life is a journey, not a final destination.

When I visit Kevin's grave, I often think "Why come here?" Standing over the headstone of the double plot that marks Kevin and now my mom's life and legacy, I am taken to the edge of eternity reminding myself there will come a day when I will be a memory too.

Bob and I often reflect on the many years we have been together. A couple since we were 15 years old, we have been married 57 years at the time I am finishing this book. As our life together winds down, we often say, "It all went by so fast. We are closer to the finish line with every day that passes. Our life's journey is almost over. We are close to our eternal home."

What do you know or believe about life after death? Do you have the hope of Eternity? Are you staying in your lane, pressing on toward what will be your final destination? Are you like a ship tossed in a storm, a wave crashing against the rocks? Do you feel lost?

Seeking, acknowledging, accepting, and embracing the truth that this life is not all there is keeps me looking ahead rather than behind. None of us know how much time is left for us here on this earth. Cemeteries are full of those who wish they had more time. The time I have left might come to an end at any moment. Because so many people dear to me have died, and mostly the death of my son, I have moved much closer to living at the edge of eternity. Heaven seems more real and closer than ever before, and because I know God, I know peace—*"which surpasses all understanding"* (Philippians 4:7, ESV). As are redemption and salvation, God's peace is a gift—a byproduct of hope and faith. All we have to do is ask, and He will freely give His peace.

If you do not know God, and you haven't invited Him into your heart, your life, and your grieving, I hope you will do that right now. It's really very simple. *"Ask and you shall receive"* (Matthew 7:7–8).

Living fully in the here and now, I nevertheless eagerly anticipate the time when it's my turn to enter Heaven's gates. The joy of seeing my dad, my mom, my brother, Kevin, and all those who will go on before me brings me great joy.

I imagine it will be Kevin who will move toward me with the others following him. He will be more beautiful than I remembered, surrounded by soft white light, and his eyes will reflect a dance of lights that mirrors his soul. He will smile his signature smile with his arms reaching out to me. When we hold each other, he will melt into my arms as he did as a child. We will just hold each other for a while, and then he will whisper something to me like, "Hey, Mom. I've missed you. I'm so glad to see you. There's someone waiting to meet you."

My family and friends gather around me saying words like, "We've missed you. We never stopped loving you. It was hard to say goodbye, but it seems like it's only been a few minutes since we were together. We've been waiting for you, and so has He."

Taking my hand in his, Kevin and I will walk on the "*street of the city [of] gold, as pure as transparent glass*" (Revelation 21:21, NIV). I will be overwhelmed by the beauty and majesty of Heaven, angelic beings, and Heavenly creatures everywhere. I take a breath, breathing in the breath of Heaven at last. In what sounds like a chorus of praise and excitement, people in the crowd begin to shout, "I see Him. He's coming. There He is. The King is coming. The King is coming!"

Kevin and I look at each other and laugh out loud, and we begin to run toward the brilliant light before us. The crowd parts and there He will be looking at me, calling my name with His arms wide open and a smile I have no words to describe. I see His nail-scarred hands—the symbols of His sacrifice that paid the price for my redemption and the gift of eternal life.

Running faster with my arms outstretched I cry out, "Jesus! Jesus! I'm here! I'm finally here!" When He reaches me, He takes me in His arms and says, "Welcome home, my beloved. Welcome home!"

Sometimes, I can't wait!

"*Lo, I see my father and my father's father. Lo, I see my mother and my mother's mother, and my brothers and my sisters. And, I shall stand with my family with Christ forever and ever and ever.*"   —Uncle Rod Carter

"*He will wipe away every tear from your eyes. There will be no more death or mourning or crying or pain, for the old order of things has passed away.*"   (Revelation 21:4)

"*And since we are His children, we are His heirs. In fact, together with Christ we are heirs of God's glory. But if we are to share His glory, we must also share His suffering.*"
                                                    (Romans 8:17)

"*For the grace of God has appeared that offers salvation to all people. It teaches us to say, 'no' to ungodliness and worldly passions, and to live self-controlled, upright and godly lives in this present age, while we wait for the blessed hope—the appearing of the glory of our great God and Savior, Jesus Christ, who gave Himself for us to redeem us from all wickedness and to purify for Himself a people that are His very own, eager to do what is good.*"   (Titus 2:13–14)

Therefore I live for today
Certain of finding
Guidance and strength for the way.
Power for each moment of weakness.
Hope for each moment of pain,
Comfort for every sorrow. Sunshine and joy after rain.
—Anonymous

Acknowledgments

WITH MUCH LOVE AND GRATITUDE, I ACKNOWLEDGE the long list of those who made this book possible by being a significant part of my life, and my journey through grief.

To my dad and my mom, who created a home and family life built on the foundations of God's love, faithfulness, and grace. For teaching me about God the Father, the Son, and the Holy Spirit, and encouraging me to realize and accept my identity as a Daughter of the King. For all the fun we had and the many special memories I cherish. I had an amazing childhood because of you!

To my brother, Russ, who was the first boy I loved and the best brother anyone could have. He made me feel special and beautiful.

To my husband, Bob, the love of my life since I was 15 years old. For the passion and love we share and have fought for through the years. For reading, rereading, and listening to every word written in this book with an attentive ear. For being a loving dad to our three sons and their families. For never giving up on us!

To our sons, Eric, David, and Kevin, who complete me and are the best of who I am. To their wives, Vonda and Vel, and to Kevin's fiancée, Venus—our three daughters-of-the-heart born of another mother.

To our precious grandchildren and great-grandchildren who make life grand and ensure something of us will live on long after we are gone.

To my beautiful, loving, and loyal lifelong friends, Sharon and Dana. We met as children and have been friends through "thick and thin."

To my niece, Andrea Carter, and my dear friends and fellow authors, Stella Ma, Judy Cunningham, Kathe Wunnenberg, Jodi Rosser, and Anne Underwood, for your support and encouragement that kept me writing when I wanted to quit.

To Cynthia Weightman, my sister of the heart and cofounding director of "Mothers Like Me Grief Care and Support Ministry." The times we spent together comforting and encouraging grieving moms were some of the most meaningful and spiritually fruitful times of my life.

To my brother-in-law, Rod Carter, a tender warrior with a poet's heart, who introduced me to classical literature and encouraged me to read and write.

To Adam Colwell of Write Works for encouraging me to go deeper, which improved and changed the way I write. If it wasn't for him, the manuscript would still be in a folder on my desk. To Joni Wilson, editor, for her finishing touches before the manuscript became a book.

To the many teachers, authors, pastors, spiritual leaders, professional, and spiritual mentors whose words and examples have challenged, inspired, and motivated me to study God's Word and to mature in Christ.

To God the Father, Son, and Holy Spirit for Your love and faithfulness. You are the breath of Heaven (Psalm 33:6) and the wind that causes me to fly with broken wings!

To my son, Kevin Russell, the "warming fire who leaned against me and touched my very soul." You knew at a very young age how to love unconditionally. Your death turned up the heat that tested, refined, and purified my heart and soul and strengthened my faith. "I love you, son. I will see you soon!"

"Death takes the body. God takes the soul. Our mind holds the memories. Our hearts keep the love. Our faith lets us know we will meet again." —Unknown

Words of Hope from the Word of God

"I pray that the eyes of your heart may be enlightened in order that you may know the hope to which He has called you, the riches of His glorious inheritance in His holy people."

(Ephesians 1:18)

"But those who hope in the LORD will renew their strength. They will soar on wings like eagles; they will run and not grow weary, they will walk and not be faint."

(Isaiah 40:31)

"Hope deferred makes the heart sick (and crushes the spirit); but a longing fulfilled is a tree of life."

(Proverbs 13:12)

"And hope does not put us to shame because God's love has been poured out into our hearts through the Holy Spirit, who has given to us."

(Romans 5:5)

"Be joyful in hope, patient in affliction, faithful in prayer."

(Romans 12:12)

"But blessed is the one who trusts in the LORD, whose confidence is in Him. They will be like a tree planted by the water that sends out its roots by the stream. It does not fear when heat comes; its leaves are always green. It has no worries in a year of drought and never fails to bear fruit."

(Jeremiah 17:7)

"I say to myself, The LORD is my portion; therefore I will wait for Him. The LORD is good to those whose hope is in Him, to the one who seeks Him."

(Lamentations 3:24–25)

"Seek the LORD your God, you will find Him, if you seek Him with all your heart and with all your soul . . . for the LORD your God is a merciful God; He will not abandon you."

(Deuteronomy 4:29–30)

"Move your heart closer and closer to God and He will come closer to you. But, make sure you cleanse your life, you sinner, and keep your heart pure and stop doubting."

(Jeremiah 11:3)

"Come near to God and He will come near to you."

(James 4:8)

"Hear me, LORD, and answer me, for I am poor and needy . . .
Hear my prayer, LORD, listen to my cry for mercy. When I
am in distress, I call to You, because You answer me."

(Psalm 86:1–7)

"Be merciful to me, Lord, for I am in distress; my eyes grow
weak with sorrow, my soul and body with grief. My life is
consumed by anguish and my years by groaning; my strength
fails because of my affliction and my bones grow weak."

(Psalm 31:9–10)

"Hear my cry for mercy as I call to You for help,
as I lift my hands toward Your Most Holy Place."

(Psalm 28:2)

"When you call Me, I will answer you . . I will be with you
in trouble, I will rescue you and honor you."

(Psalm 91:15, paraphrased)

"Be strong and take heart, all who hope in the Lord."

(Psalm 31:24)

"If I rise on the wings of the dawn, if I settle on the far side of
the sea, even there Your hand will guide me. Your right hand
will hold me fast."

(Psalm 139:9)

"He heals the brokenhearted and binds up their wounds."

(Psalm 147:3)

"There is surely a future and a hope for you, and your hope will not be cut off."

(Proverbs 23:18)

"For I know the plans I have for you declares the LORD, plans to prosper you and not to harm you, plans to give you hope and a future."

(Jeremiah 29:11)

"The Lord will guide you always; He will satisfy your needs . . . You will be like a well-watered garden, like a spring whose waters never fail."

(Isaiah 58:11)

"As for God, His way is perfect: The LORD's word is flawless; He shields all who take refuge in Him."

(Psalm 18:30)

"I will send down showers in season; there will be showers of blessing."

(Ezekiel 34:26)

"The people walking in darkness have seen a great light; on those living in the land of deep darkness a light has dawned."

(Isaiah 9:2)

"You turned my wailing into dancing, You removed my sack-cloth and clothed me with joy."

(Psalm 30:11)

"He has sent me to bind up the brokenhearted . . . to comfort all who mourn . . to bestow on them a crown of beauty instead of ashes, the oil of joy instead of mourning, and a garment of praise instead of a spirit of despair. beauty for ashes, the oil of joy for mourning, praise for the spirit of heaviness that they might be called trees of righteousness, the planting of the LORD that He might be glorified."

(Isaiah 61:3)

"He has made everything beautiful in His time."

(Ecclesiastes 3:11)

"Let us hold unswervingly to the hope we profess, for He who promised is faithful."

(Hebrews 10:23)

"And, the God of all grace, who called you to His eternal glory in Christ, after you have suffered a little while, will Himself restore you and make you strong, firm and steadfast. To Him be the power forever and ever. Amen."

(1 Peter 5:10)

"The LORD gives strength to His people; the LORD blesses His people with peace."

(Psalm 29:11)

"May the God of hope fill you with all joy and peace as you trust in Him, so that you may overflow with hope by the power of the Holy Spirit."

(Romans 15:13)

About the Author

ANGIE IS RETIRED AND LIVES WITH HER HUSBAND, Bob, in Northern Colorado. Born in the South, moving to the East Coast as a child, and living in Southern California for 50+ years, she has always been comfortable with change and finding joy in something new and different. With a passion for living life with meaning and purpose, she would say she is blessed, and her greatest blessings call her wife, mother, and MiMi (grandchildren and great-grandchildren).

Writing for business, education, and ministry for decades, Angie didn't discover she had the potential or skillset to be a published author until she started writing songs and children's stories.

In 2023, she coauthored and published her first book, *Little Lucy Ladybug Where Are My Spots* with Judy Cunningham, an award-winning watercolor artist. During the writing of that book, Angie and Judy formed a partnership of Cunningham and Green to create and publish a series of children's books. The publishing of their first book catapulted Angie into the world of storytellers and provided the confidence she needed to continue to write.

A Mother Like Me—A Story of Faith, Hope, and Love in Loss was in the making for 20 years after the sudden cardiac death of Angie's youngest son, Kevin, in January 2002. In 2019, she heard a story about Margaret Mitchell, the author of *Gone with the Wind*. She had broken her ankle, and her husband told her to "Write a book to entertain yourself." *A Mother Like Me* was written during the lockdowns caused by the COVID pandemic, not to entertain Angie, but it was a cathartic and therapeutic experience for her.

Angie was talented—groomed and trained to be a performing artist—but it was always writing she preferred over performing. A published songwriter, author, Bible study leader, speaker, and spiritual mentor, she is very acquainted with grief, beginning with the death of her dad when she was 12 years old. Through the years, she has suffered the loss of not only her dad and her son, Kevin, but also her stepsister, mom, brother, and many others she has deeply loved.

During her time at the bedside of those who were dying, and at the edge the grave, she learned a great deal about the journey of grief and how it affects our heart, soul, mind, and body.

Soon after the death of her son, she began to comfort, encourage, and support hundreds of grieving mothers she refers to as "mothers like me." The primary reason for writing *A Mother Like Me* is to reach out to more hurting moms in more places.

"I write words on a page to better understand myself and the world around me. The more I write, the more comfortable I am in the unchartered, unexplored territory of storytelling—a place where I know I belong." —Angie

www.ingramcontent.com/pod-product-compliance
Lightning Source LLC
Chambersburg PA
CBHW051305120626
46547CB00015B/2091